KU-652-644

the ancient islands

the ancient islands

New Zealand's natural environments

Photographs: Brian Enting
Text: Les Molloy

Port Nicholson Press
1982

Dedication
To our wives and children

Acknowledgements

In preparing this book we have been privileged to be able to draw on the knowledge of many people familiar with New Zealand's natural history. In particular, our effort has been inspired by the ecological writings of the late Leonard Cockayne, and, subsequently, those of Charles Fleming, Graeme Stevens and Peter Wardle. Without their work, our understanding of New Zealand's biogeography would be so much poorer.

It is our special pleasure to thank Tony Druce for his detailed identification of ferns, conifers and flowering plants. Ian Atkinson also provided helpful comments on parts of the text. Anne Bell drew Figure 3, and the assistance of the Department of Lands and Survey in preparing the maps is gratefully acknowledged.

We are indebted to the following people and organisations for their help, encouragement and forebearance: Nancy Adams, Gideon Anderson, Sandy Bartle, Anne and Ben Bell, John Braggins, Brian Brake, John Campbell, Shane Cotter, Peter Daniel, R. R. Forster, George Gibbs, Allan Green, Geoff Kelly, Alan Mark, Geoff Mason, Elsa Matich, Mike Meads, Ray Mole, Dave Sim, Marie Taylor, the Forest Research Institute, the staff of the Mt Bruce Bird Reserve, and the Otorohanga Zoological Society.

Our final debt is acknowledged in the dedication.

Published by the Port Nicholson Press Limited,
P.O. Box 11-838, Wellington, New Zealand

PRELIMINARY PHOTOGRAPHS:
Lichen and algae; Giant petrel, *Macronectes halli*; *Drosera auriculata*

Edited by Bridget Williams
Designed by Lindsay Missen

Printed and bound by Whitcoulls Limited,
Christchurch, New Zealand

ISBN 0 908635 04 4

Contents

Foreword

From the beginning of human occupation of the ancient islands now called New Zealand, people have treasured the experience of its landscapes, their plant cover and animal life.

In Maori tradition the colonists of the Arawa canoe discarded their tropical feather head-dresses for pohutukawa blossom. The forests provided timber for canoes and housing, birds and fruit for food, and the earth itself yielded raw materials for stone tools and weapons. When Maui the demigod lay exhausted after his struggle with the sun, the kokako brought him refreshment, and was rewarded with strong legs for leaping through the forest: the sun and the birds were partners in man's tradition and culture.

The earliest European visitors responded warmly to the bellbird's dawn chorus, the 'shrill notes of the thrushes', 'the graver pipe of the wattle-birds' and the prospect of 'rude sceneries . . . of antediluvian forests which cloathed the rock'. While the settlers laboured to clear the land for crops and pasture, many of them also recognised the beauty of the forests. Almost all of these pioneers, missionaries, explorers, sealers, settlers and traders were naturalists at heart, though only a few left written testimony of their feeling for the land – a land already being modified by occupation and commercial exploitation. As the century of European settlement drew to a close, scientists joined settlers like H. Guthrie-Smith and lovers of the outdoors like A. P. Harper in an attempt to conserve what was left, in island sanctuaries, reserves, and national parks. Pioneer photographers left a record in black and white of a land that was changing for ever, and the first generation of nature photographers – Guthrie-Smith, Edgar Stead, Leonard Cockayne and Tudor Collins – did likewise for many birds and forests.

The twentieth century has led to many specialised publications, dealing in detail with parts of the natural scene – C. A. Cotton's geomorphology, Cockayne's vegetation, Walter Buller's and other bird books, to name but a few. More recently there has been increasing emphasis on ecological relationships, and at least two symposia on the natural history and ecology of New Zealand, collecting in separate chapters the work of different authors.

In *The Ancient Islands* two young New Zealanders have joined forces to produce a book for people who have no technical training but wish to know more about the landscapes, plants and animals of the countryside. Both have brought to the task the enthusiasm of skilled naturalists, lovers of the outdoors, determined to ensure that these distinctive characteristics of New Zealand shall remain, despite inevitable change, the 'key signature' of their homeland. They are dedicated to the objective of capturing readers' interest and support for the conservation of the unique natural environments that are the raw material – in Aldo Leopold's wise phrase – for that product we may be tempted to call New Zealand culture.

Brian Enting and Les Molloy have collaborated so well to stimulate and supplement each other's talents, that I found it hard to believe that they had never met until they were brought together to work on this book. Their view of New Zealand is a balanced one, embracing all the diversities of coasts and islands, of lowlands and high country, of forest, wetlands, alpine fellfield and tussock grasslands, set in a time scale that stretches back to the ancient continent of Gondwanaland. The origins of New Zealand's natural environments – the fishing of Maui in twentieth-century imagery – has never been better told to the layman. It is a dramatic story that should be known to us all, the history of the land and life we inherit from the past and hold in trust for posterity.

CHARLES FLEMING

Introduction

In this book we try, through word and picture, to evoke the feeling of New Zealand's natural environments. The ecological relationships between our plants and animals and their physical surroundings are fascinating, and often little understood. We have carefully chosen examples of both typical and unusual features to illustrate these relationships. This is a selective approach, but one that we trust will stimulate readers to delve more deeply into the reasons why our plants and animals inhabit particular coastlines, forests, swamps or mountains.

Each of our natural environments consists of a number of ecosystems, that is, an interdependent community of plants and animals (mostly indigenous) living in a self-sustaining way within their physical surroundings. And within each ecosystem there is a sense of order. There are food chains involving *producers*, such as marine and land plants which accumulate the sun's energy; *primary consumers*, such as insects and herbivorous animals that consume this plant material; *secondary consumers*, such as carnivorous predators and scavengers that live upon insects or smaller animals; and *decomposers* (fungi and soil animals) that convert this complex organic matter of dead plants and animals back into their raw inorganic elements, to be cycled again as nutrients through the particular ecosystem. Using a minimum of technical terms, we aim to illustrate and explain the following concepts:

- Each plant or animal species has a favoured *ecological niche*, where it is most likely to compete effectively and complete its life cycle. Such a place is sometimes called a *habitat*, that is, a place of shelter and sustenance.
- The geographical distribution of plants and animals is not just a matter of chance – wide variations in climate, topography, rock type and soil all have a major influence on their survival. In some places, plant and animal communities have developed ways of handling periodic natural hazards – fire and volcanic activity, earthquake, flooding or landslide.
- These soil/plant/animal communities are dynamic and in particular there is a gradual, ordered change that occurs with soil development and plant succession over time, particularly on younger land forms.

There are many ways in which the natural landscapes of New Zealand could be categorised. We have looked at the environments to be found at different altitudes, from seashore to mountain top:

the off-shore and outlying islands with their relics of Gondwanaland's fauna (Chapter 2);
the coastal zone, the interface between the life of the sea and the land (Chapter 3);
lowland, montane and subalpine forests with their complex structures and life-cycles (Chapters 4 and 7);
wetlands, fertile habitats which are diminishing in extent throughout New Zealand (Chapter 5);
tussock grasslands, a major natural environment used by man for pastoral purposes (Chapter 6);
the alpine zone, rich in beautiful plant communities despite the harsh climate (Chapter 8);
the volcanic lands, some restless in their thermal activity, others bearing the imprint of eruptions of long ago (Chapter 9).

Although at times we have focused on the unique and the ancient, we believe that we have also emphasised the commonplace and cosmopolitan plants and animals, for together they give New Zealand its distinctive indigenous character. Above all, however, we hope that we have shared with our readers not just wonder at the beauty and order of creation, but also a sense of urgency, a realisation that these areas are now only remnants of the once-pristine natural environments of primitive New Zealand. They are a priceless heritage, worthy of our interest and concern, inviting endeavours to conserve them.

LES MOLLOY & BRIAN ENTING

CHAPTER ONE

Ancient New Zealand

SILVER FERN, *Cyathea dealbata*

'Observe the young and tender frond of this punga: shaped and curved like the scroll of a fiddle: fit instrument to play archaic tunes.'
A. R. D. Fairburn

To describe New Zealand as 'the ancient islands' may at first seem paradoxical. We are a young nation with a Polynesian cultural heritage of perhaps 1,200 years and only 150 odd years of European settlement. Maori legend tells of a new land, Te-ika-a-Maui, rising out of the sea long after Tane-mahuta covered Papa-tu-a-nuku, his mother the far-reaching earth, with his offspring the trees and forest birds. To the European explorers of the seventeenth and eighteenth centuries, the land must have appeared youthful and luxuriant in contrast to the worn landforms of neighbouring Australia. Tasman's 'land uplifted high' was indeed a land of young mountains: the Southern Alps and other great axial ranges have been formed only in the last 5 million years, and volcanoes are still active in the North Island. A mere 600 years before the arrival of the first Polynesians a large portion of the North Island had been totally devastated by the cataclysmic Taupo eruption which spread more than 60 cubic kilometres of rhyolitic pumice and ignimbrite over the centre of the North Island, incinerating the forest and remoulding the landscape.

But the origins of New Zealand's landforms and many of its plants and animals reach back far beyond these times. Some of the plants and animals that excited Captain Cook's naturalists were of great antiquity – the southern beech (*Nothofagus*) forests and the podocarp forests with their profusion of ferns; animals such as the tuatara, so often called 'a living fossil'; the native frogs of the ancient genus *Leiopelma*, and the twilight birds, kiwi and kakapo; *Peripatus*, the creature like a half-caterpillar/half-worm that is a relic of an ancient group of animals that appeared on earth 500 million years ago. Few of us now live in sight of these once great forests, let alone ever see a live native frog, tuatara or kakapo. Yet there are relics of the biota of ancient New Zealand all around us, from the weta in the woodpile to the tree fern at the bottom of the garden.

THE ANCIENT NEW ZEALAND LANDMASS: The evolutionary story of New Zealand is a fascinating one and, of course, it hasn't ended yet. There are still many enigmas that lack an adequate explanation. However, we know much more now than we did 20, or even 10, years ago through the concept called 'plate tectonics', which has revolutionised our understanding of the world's biogeographical history. Plate tectonics describes the creation of global features (such as continents, seas and mountain ranges) through the movement of 'plates' of the earth's crust. Its analysis of spreading in the sea floor, which in turn leads to the jostling of the plates like a massive jigsaw, has greatly amplified and largely supplanted earlier theories like 'continental drift'. Volcanic activity is a feature of the edges of the plates, and the mechanisms underlying the formation and destruction of plates are discussed in more detail in Chapter 9.

In the simplest sense, New Zealand has been formed through a complicated chain of events occurring over the last 300 million years at the junction of two of these plates – the Indian-Australian and the Pacific. In the middle of the Carboniferous period (Fig. 1) the site of modern New Zealand was a sea basin wedged between the coasts of eastern Australia and Antarctica – two parts of the ancient supercontinent of Gondwanaland which consisted of the continents of Africa, India, South America, Australia and Antarctica (Fig. 2). For the next 150 million years, until late Jurassic times, this basin was a vast dumping ground for sand and silt eroded from the surrounding continents. These layers of sediment were gradually compressed into hard sandstones and siltstones (greywacke and argillites) of enormous thickness, reaching down tens of kilometres in places.

This long period of underwater deposition ended abruptly about 140 to 120 million years ago, during the late Jurassic and early Cretaceous periods. At about this time, a major collision between continental masses on the two plates caused much of the sea floor to be thrust up out of the sea, along with volcanic material and some of the earth's mantle (Chapter 9), to become the ancestral New Zealand landmass. But Gondwanaland had already begun to break up and ancestral New Zealand was caught up in plate movements that ultimately resulted in New Zealand becoming a group of isolated islands in the South Pacific Ocean (Chapter 2).

FIGURE 1:
Summary of major events in New Zealand during the last 350 million years of geological time.

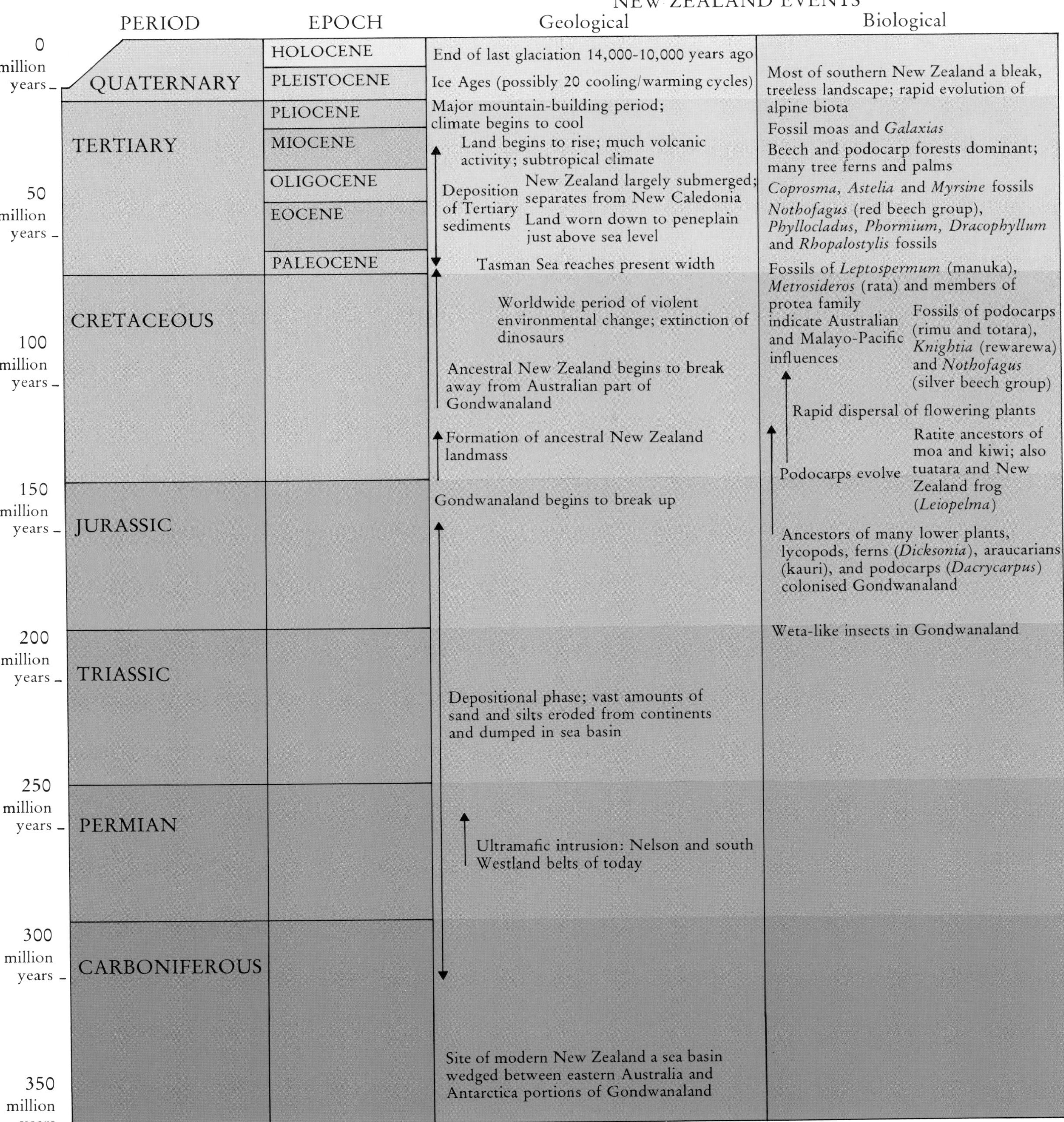

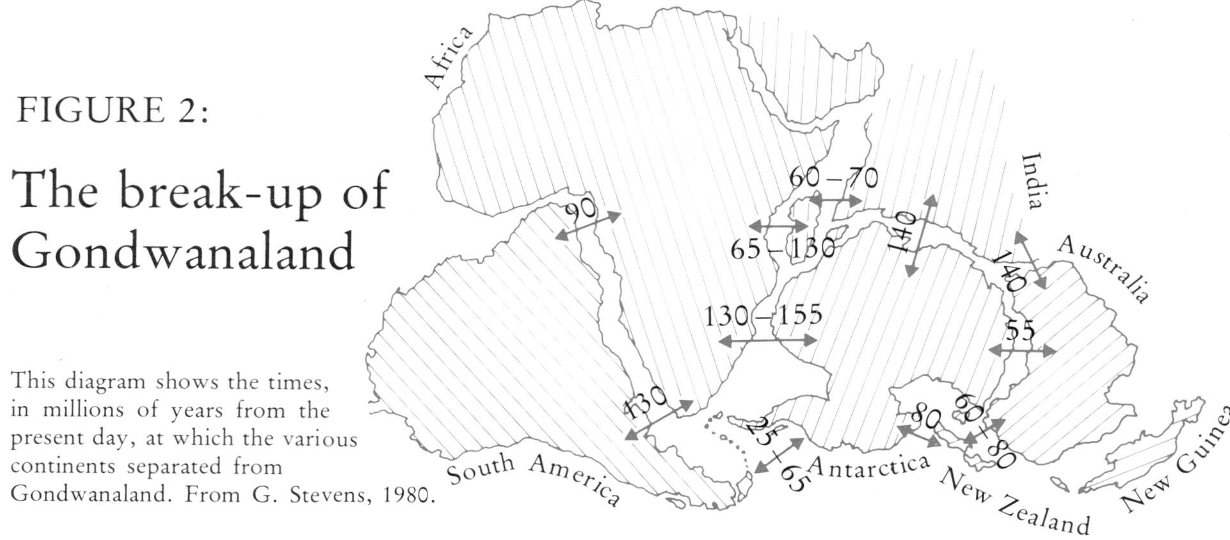

FIGURE 2:

The break-up of Gondwanaland

This diagram shows the times, in millions of years from the present day, at which the various continents separated from Gondwanaland. From G. Stevens, 1980.

PERIPATUS
Peripatus, Peripatoides novaezealandiae, *is a relic of a very ancient and curious group of animals which is still widespread in the southern hemisphere countries that once made up the supercontinent of Gondwanaland. Peripatus has characteristics of both insects and worms. A very small creature (only 3-4 cm long), it inhabits the damp forest floor and preys upon spiders and insects. These are usually ensnared in a jet of viscous fluid emitted from the mouth.*

GONDWANALAND AND THE ORIGIN OF NEW ZEALAND'S BIOTA: The unusual flora and fauna of modern New Zealand are a direct result of the timing of the separation of the ancestral New Zealand landmass from the rest of Gondwanaland. By the Jurassic period (around 180 million years ago) the ancestors of our ferns (the tree ferns, for instance, and *Blechnum*, the common hard ferns) and the kauri had colonised Gondwanaland; mammals had not yet evolved, so reptiles, amphibians and the first birds roamed the land. A specialised group of conifers (podocarps) with greatly reduced cones gradually evolved and established themselves in Gondwanaland along with the araucarian forests (ancestors of the kauri). One of the most ancient, the genus *Dacrycarpus*, was present 110 million years ago and is still represented in New Zealand today by the tallest of our magnificent podocarps, kahikatea.

By the middle of the Cretaceous period (110-80 million years ago) the character of New Zealand's modern forests was ensured: the primitive ancestors of not only kauri, kahikatea, rimu and totara but also silver beech (*Nothofagus menziesii*), rewarewa (*Knightia*) and another widespread relative of the podocarp family, *Phyllocladus*, were established. During this period ancestral New Zealand began to break away from the Australian part of Gondwanaland as a rift formed in what is now the Tasman Sea. Plants and animals needing a land-bridge could no longer migrate to New Zealand. However, subsequent sea floor spreading in the Tasman Sea probably did not begin until late Cretaceous times (80 million years ago) and ceased when the Tasman Sea reached its present width (1,800 km) 60 million years ago. So it is possible that some plants and animals could still migrate to New Zealand up until the end of the Cretaceous period by island-hopping or rafting across the narrow Tasman Sea.

Ancient New Zealand was launched into the southern oceans with biota uniquely her own. Monotremes (platypus-like animals), marsupials and snakes were left behind in Australia. The only mammal in this archaic fauna was the short-tailed bat (*Mystacina*). In the absence of mammalian predators, many of the ecological niches filled by mammals elsewhere in the world were exploited by birds. The ratite birds (moas and kiwis) were probably already flightless, and some of the moas evolved into giants up to 3.5 m in height. By living both in the forest and at the more open forest edge, they successfully filled the niche usually occupied by mammalian herbivores (sheep, cattle and deer); the smaller moas and kiwis tended to browse the forest undergrowth or develop specialised organs for nocturnal probing of the forest floor. It has even been suggested that heavy browsing by moas led to divarication (development of a twiggy juvenile form) in many New Zealand trees and shrubs, as a type of 'defence mechanism'. Other birds, such as the kakapo, takahe and weka, also lost the power of flight in this predator-free environment. The 'genetic relaxation' that took place among the birds is generally indicated by: a tendency to grow larger; feathers becoming heavier and sparser; and melanism (the loss of colour patterns, usually a reversion to black) in birds such as shags, wekas, oystercatchers, fantails and robins.

Evolution of lower forms of life in ancient New Zealand likewise reflects the absence of mammalian predators. Our insect fauna is vast in numbers of species, and it includes a rich population of flightless, ground-surface insects, many related to insects in those southern countries that were once part of Gondwanaland. Among the most ancient are the wetas, which have been aptly termed 'insect rodents' because, in their diet and nocturnal lifestyle, they have filled the ecological niche usually occupied by mice.

There are many other interesting relics of this Gondwanaland flora and fauna:

- the beautiful, large native land-snails, including *Paryphanta* with its coiled shell over 8 cm in diameter
- the ancient reptiles, not only the remarkable tuatara but also the geckos which show many primitive features and are likely to be related to genera in New Caledonia (which probably separated from New Zealand at the beginning of the Oligocene epoch, around 37 million years ago)
- the native frogs of the genus *Leiopelma* (Hochstetter's frog, Archey's frog and the very rare Hamilton's frog), with their primitive characteristics: no tadpole stage; tail muscles but no tail; no webbing between toes; and the ability to inhabit a range of forest and grassland environments, as they do not seem to need running or standing water for survival
- curious plants – the Psilotales, *Tmesipteris* (several species) and *Psilotum nudum*, which are not ferns but 'living fossils', relics of a very ancient division of the plant kingdom.

It is truly remarkable that so many of these plants and animals from Gondwanaland survived the turbulent events of the subsequent 80 million years of geological history (Fig. 1.2) – climatic change, uplift and submergence, earthquakes and volcanic activity. The pace of environmental change quickened after the onset of a major mountain-building period in the Pliocene (5–2 million years ago) leading to the formation of most of the axial mountain ranges and 'basin and range' topography (such as Central Otago or the Grey–Inangahua Depression on the West Coast). Then, during the so-called Pleistocene Ice Ages (2 million to 14,000 years ago), the land and its biota had to endure severe climatic oscillations, a series of cold periods alternating with warmer periods. At the peak of the last glaciation (Otiran), 20,000–18,000 years ago, glaciers and snowfields covered these relatively new mountain ranges – the Southern Alps, Kaikouras and the higher mountains in the southern North Island. As the soil and vegetation was stripped from the higher land, huge outwash plains of river gravels formed in the Canterbury Plains and in the area (now drowned by the sea) between the Manawatu and Tasman Bay in Nelson.

HOCHSTETTER'S FROG
Hochstetter's frog, Leiopelma hochstetteri, *is more common than New Zealand's two other rare native frogs – Archey's frog and Hamilton's frog. Unlike these two, this frog is often found close to water, particularly on streambanks in the Coromandel and Kaimai Ranges. All three are members of the ancient genus* Leiopelma.

NATIVE LAND SNAIL
The beautiful large land snails of the genus Paryphanta *are relics of Gondwanaland's fauna. Populations of* Paryphanta *have been isolated in the ridge-top refuges of the mountains and forests of north-west Nelson by the glaciations of the Pleistocene Ice Ages. Subsequently, separate subspecies have evolved.*

POST-GLACIAL NEW ZEALAND: Many of the ancient plants and animals, and particularly some of the birds, were probably wiped out during the Ice Ages (although many migratory birds probably began their seasonal visitations during this period). As the glaciers began to retreat and the climate began to warm up at the end of the last glaciation, 14,000 to 10,000 years ago, the youthful landforms would have offered many new habitats for these surviving plants and animals, or new immigrants. Remaining areas of exposed sea floor, glacial and river terraces, fans and valley floors, and moraines would all have been open to colonisation by various forms of plant life. Studies of the vegetation on the landforms of different ages adjacent to the Fox and Franz Josef Glaciers (on the humid western side of the Southern Alps) and the Mueller, Hooker and Tasman Glaciers (on the drier eastern side) tell a fascinating story of plant succession today. Similar processes would probably have occurred as the glaciers of the Ice Ages waned.

Some of the bare rock would have been covered by lichens whose secretions can slowly dissolve the surface minerals. Finer debris (sand and gravels) would have supported mosses (such as *Racomitrium*) and tufts of short grasses (*Poa, Rytidosperma*), cushion mats (*Raoulia*) or hardy herbs (such as the many species of willow herb, *Epilobium*). Because these rudimentary, mineral soils would have lacked humus, nitrogen-fixing plants such as the native brooms (*Carmichaelia*) and tutu (*Coriaria*) would have played an important colonising role. After 100–200 years a dense growth of shrubs (*Dracophyllum*, *Phyllocladus*, *Hebe*, or snow totara) would have covered the surface in the wetter areas, while scattered groves of the prickly wild irishman (*Discaria toumatou*) would have predominated in more arid regions. At higher altitudes (above 1,000 m) a dense growth of tall snow tussocks (*Chionochloa*) would have established itself in about 300 years, along with a rich flora of herbaceous plants – the mountain daisies (*Celmisia*), wild spaniards (*Aciphylla*) and mountain buttercups (*Ranunculus*). A low forest of wineberry, ribbonwood, Hall's totara, broadleaf, rata, kamahi and many other smaller trees would probably cover the lower slopes after 300 years. The final stage, the tall podocarp forests of rimu, totara, miro or matai, would have

BLACK STILT
The black stilt, Himanotopus novaezealandiae, *shares the dubious honour with the kakapo and takahe of being one of New Zealand's rarest mainland birds – and it is probably the rarest species of wader in the world. Less than a hundred birds survive in the river beds, deltas and lakes of the Mackenzie Basin. Their decline has probably been due to predation by ferrets and cats as well as the destruction of many nesting areas by development for the generation of hydro-electricity.*

TUATARA
The tuatara, Sphenodon punctatus, *is the most notable representative of New Zealand's ancient fauna. Tuatara can truly be called a 'living fossil', for it is the only living relic of the otherwise extinct order of reptiles called the Rynchocephalia which dates back to Gondwanaland during the lower Triassic, 220 million years ago. The tuatara is considered rare (although not endangered); it is no longer present on the mainland but can be found on at least 30 offshore islands in Cook Strait and around the north-eastern coast of the North Island.*

taken several hundred more years, depending upon the climatic and soil conditions of each particular region.

But not all parts of New Zealand were swept clean of vegetation by the glaciers, or ravaged by the volcanic activity which produced new landforms in so much of the central North Island. Forests, shrubs and grasslands survived in the far north, eastern parts of the South Island, Stewart Island and, curiously enough, two widely separated but geologically similar parts of the western South Island – north-west Nelson and Fiordland. These two mountainous regions were both important refuges for plants, particularly many alpine plants and beech forests. Whereas the podocarps are rapidly dispersed (because their seeds sit on top of fleshy, coloured receptacles which are eaten by birds), beech nuts are unpalatable to birds, too heavy for wind dispersal, and are most successfully distributed by floating down waterways. Consequently, beech forests are still slowly invading some of the lowland podocarp forests from the mountain strongholds of Fiordland and north-west Nelson.

These examples indicate the type of revegetation likely in a mountainous land with a temperate (or even cool-temperate) climate. For that is exactly what most of New Zealand is. Most New Zealanders now live in cities close to the coast with its milder climate. It is all too easy to forget that post-glacial New Zealand really is a very rugged mountainous land, with nearly half of the country consisting of steepland (that is, land with slopes greater than 28°), much of which lies above 300 m in altitude. These mountain ranges also act as barriers to the prevailing, moisture-laden westerly winds. The leeward (eastern) regions of the country generally experience a drier climate and would have carried a more open, dryland forest association of kanuka, black beech and totara/matai. In the very dry, inland basins of Central Otago, the Waitaki and inland Marlborough, the climate is more severe, almost 'continental' with cold, frosty winters and hot, dry summers. In such fire-prone areas, woody shrubs and low tussock grasslands would have been induced through periodic natural fires.

But this 'rain-shadow' vegetation is the consequence of only one set of climatic and topographical features. In post-glacial times, as in modern New Zealand, there were many different natural habitats. Climate acted in a number of ways on different land forms and different soils. There was considerable variety in soil parent materials, that is, raw materials such as weathered rock (of different geological composition), loess (wind-blown dust), volcanic ash, alluvium (river sediments), organic matter (peat). Some landforms were young, others had existed long enough to have a significant cover of soil and vegetation. Topography varied greatly throughout the land, with the periodic rejuvenation of soils on steeper slopes or flood-plains contrasting with the older soils on more stable surfaces such as glacial terraces. Rock types were of several kinds of chemical composition: sedimentary rocks such as the hard greywacke and argillite were most common, underlying many of the axial mountain ranges; softer sedimentary rocks such as 'papa' (mudstone) were younger; acid (silica-rich) igneous rocks such as the very hard, coarse-grained rock, granite, had been crystallised slowly from the earth's magma and predominated in the old landscapes of Fiordland and north-west Nelson. In other areas metamorphic rocks such as schist and gneiss had been exposed on the surface long after they had been recrystallised under high pressure or temperature from other rocks. This diversity in rock, soil, climate and topography created the vast range of landforms and plant/animal communities that characterised these islands at the time the first human beings arrived.

THE IMPACT OF MAN: The New Zealand that confronted the first Polynesian immigrants 1,200 years ago was mostly covered in forest. The remaining 20 per cent of the land included the alpine zone, a limited area of semi-arid land in Central Otago, and grasslands such as the red tussock lands of the central North Island volcanoes and the Southland plains. Beech forests were probably still recolonising some of the tussock basins of inland Canterbury, and peatland vegetation would have covered much of the Waikato, Hauraki Plains and the Chatham Islands.

Much of the dryland forest in the eastern parts of both islands was probably destroyed by the fires of the early Polynesians. In its place there developed a short tussock grassland, so characteristic of the drier parts of Canterbury, Otago and inland Marlborough. By the time Europeans began to colonise New Zealand, probably only 50 per cent of the land was left under forest and this has been systematically reduced to only 23 per cent (primarily higher altitude, steepland forests) over the past 150 years of settlement.

Whereas the rural landscape of Europe evolved during thousands of years of human habitation, in colonial New Zealand this process was greatly accelerated by settlers unfamiliar with the climate, soils, plants and animals of a new land. Natural resources such as seals and the kauri forests were ruthlessly exploited. The introduction, through ignorance or sentiment, of undesirable Old World plants and animals caused widespread disruption. Rabbits, possums, deer, goats, stoats and rodents, gorse, broom, heather, briar and nasella tussock – all wrought havoc in both indigenous and agricultural ecosystems. In regions such as the Canterbury/Marlborough high country and the hill country of the East Cape, the removal of forest by burning and subsequent overgrazing contributed to serious, accelerated erosion, particularly of soils derived from greywacke detritus and soft sedimentary rocks. The soil erosion was widespread and obvious; less noticeable was the loss of many unique plant communities and the destruction of habitats for native fauna, through the clearing of forests, drainage of swamps and the repeated burning of tussock grasslands.

FALLOW DEER
*The first of these deer were introduced as early as 1864. But, unlike red deer, fallow deer (*Dama dama*) are slow colonisers and tend to stay close to their points of liberation. They prefer open river flats and penetrate to the bushline infrequently. As a result, they have been less of a pest than red deer.*

This destruction of habitats has contributed greatly to the extinction of many native bird species. Not only did the early Polynesians exterminate the moa, but the ecological changes they caused probably also led to the extinction of a host of other, lesser-known birds – an eagle, several rails, the New Zealand coot, a crow, a pelican and two harriers, to name just some. European colonisation continued and quickened the process. Many naturalists consider that parasites and diseases introduced by exotic birds added to the more obvious damage done by the competition and predation of animals brought by the colonists. Whatever the reasons, many more birds – including the New Zealand thrush, the huia, the New Zealand quail, the laughing owl and many subspecies of rail, snipe and wren – have gone. Sadly, the impact of man has been most severe for the more distinctive part of the fauna – the older species, most of them now found only in New Zealand.

But the ecological influence of European settlement has been even more devastating than this: the native forests and other indigenous habitats have been essentially displaced from the lowlands by grass/clover pastures or pine forests, where only a limited number of native animals, let alone plants, have managed to survive. The indigenous flora and fauna is now largely confined to the more intractable parts of the landscape – gullies, steepland, some wetlands and remote or extremely wet, infertile lowlands such as central Westland, south-east Otago or western Southland. It is estimated that only half of one per cent of New Zealand's land area has been designated a national park or reserve where the land also had a potential for production. Our attitudes towards the preservation of this natural heritage have reflected the utilitarian values of a pioneer society; until recently, there has been very little real economic sacrifice.

THE ENDEMIC REMNANTS: The notable characteristic of this native flora and fauna is their high degree of endemism – that is, they are confined to this group of islands only. Table 1 shows that most of the native species of plants and animals still living today belong exclusively to New Zealand.

TABLE I: New Zealand native flora and fauna

	Number of living species native to New Zealand	Percentage of species that are endemic
Higher plants	1,980–2,100	81
Terrestrial birds	65	57
Reptiles	*c.* 38	100
Amphibians	3	100
Fish (freshwater)	25–26	85
Arthropods (insects, etc.)	20,000 approx.	> 90
Mammals (terrestrial)	2	100

Reproduced from L. F. Molloy (ed.), 1980.

LAUGHING OWL
This nocturnal owl, Sceloglaux albifacies, *is much larger than the morepork. It was once widespread, particularly in the more open, eastern parts of both islands. Early European explorers described its loud cry as a series of dismal shrieks. Now the laughing owl is probably extinct, its indigenous habitat almost eliminated through burning and pastoral development.*

HUIA
Male (upper), *female* (lower). *The huia* (Heteralocha acutirostris) *was probably most common in montane beech forests such as those of the Tararua, Ruahine and Rimutaka Ranges. The birds worked in pairs, the male chiselling away at rotten logs and the female probing for grubs with her slender curvèd beak. Now this most notable of New Zealand's forest birds is extinct, the victim of predators and human vanity.*

Many of the endemic birds are distinctive species, probably of ancient origin, while some are relatively recent arrivals and still retain affinities with other birds, usually Australian. In the latter category are birds such as the banded rail, brown duck, fantail, pipit and kingfisher. The pukeko is clearly a more recent immigrant than our other rail, the endangered takahe, and our bellbird and stitchbird both share characteristics with the Australian honeyeaters. The origin of other birds, such as the *Nestor* parrots (the present kea and kaka), wrybill, blue duck and tui, is not so clear since they have probably been here long enough (millions or even tens of millions of years) to evolve into distinctive New Zealand genera.

A few endemic birds, however, stand out as representatives of our biological heritage by virtue of their antiquity and their evolution into unusual forms. The kiwi rightly deserves to be chosen as national emblem since it is the most ancient of the New Zealand birds, a link back to the extinct moas and the great forests of Gondwanaland. The large flightless parrot, the kakapo, is possibly even more distinctive and certainly rarer – currently one of the world's most endangered birds (as well as being one of the largest known parrots). The only member of an endemic genus, it has survived in two small populations in extremely remote mountainous parts of southern New Zealand: there are perhaps fewer than 10 birds in Fiordland (with no known females) and fewer than 100 on Stewart Island. The resonant booming sound emitted by the males in their attempts to attract the limited number of female birds can be heard up to 5 km away on a still night. Anyone fortunate enough to hear this eerie call in these uninhabited mountains has truly experienced something of primaeval New Zealand. It forms part of a courtship pattern known as 'arena behaviour', a polygamous mating system (similar to that exhibited by deer) whereby a few dominant males briefly mate with the female birds and the males then play no further part in feeding or nesting. This type of behaviour is a feature of the bowerbirds and birds of paradise in New Guinea but is not known in any other New Zealand birds. Not only is the kakapo the only known flightless arena-bird, but it is also probably the only example of a bird evolving this curious behaviour in an environment that lacked mammalian predators.

There are three other families among our endemic birds which also indicate the antiquity of our native fauna, since their ancestors probably arrived in the early Tertiary period (40–65 million years ago). They are the New Zealand wrens (including the diminutive rifleman, and the rock, bush and Stephens Island wrens), the native thrush (piopio), and the beautiful wattlebirds (the saddleback, kokako and the huia). The native thrush and the Stephens Island and bush wrens are probably now extinct; the other two small wrens (the rifleman and the rock wren) inhabit remote montane beech forests and alpine herbfields. Their cheerful acrobatics charm mountaineers and naturalists alike, but they are rarely seen by most nature lovers and are probably not widely recognised as distinctive members of our native fauna. Rather it is the wattlebirds which have taken on a symbolic importance for conservationists, for they can claim both antiquity and an association with the remnants of the once vast forests of primitive New Zealand.

The huia was probably the most notable of the wattlebirds, for its black tail feathers with their white tips were greatly esteemed by the Maoris as a symbol of high rank when worn in the *tikitiki* (top knot) on the crown of the head. In recent times, the kokako with its haunting yet melodious call has been used to symbolise the campaign to preserve its last major habitat, some of the dense podocarp forests, such as Pureora, on the volcanic plateau of the central North Island. All three wattlebirds rarely left the forest and spent a significant part of their time feeding on the forest floor; by having their wings and tail partially spread they would climb agilely to the forest canopy by a series of light hops, then glide back to the forest floor. All three birds would have been particularly vulnerable because of their poor powers of flight and preference for feeding in the lower parts of the forest. Now the huia is almost certainly extinct, exterminated in its last mountain forest retreats of the Tararua, Ruahine and Huiarau Ranges, in part by Maoris and Europeans wishing to satisfy human vanity. Similarly the saddleback has been eliminated on the mainland, probably by cats and rats, to survive only on a small number of islands.

The wattlebirds, kiwi and kakapo are notable members of our endemic fauna because of both their ancient lineages and their unique characteristics. But our concern for the preservation of the ancient and unique should not be at the expense of the more modern and commonplace plants and animals, for all have contributed in some way to New Zealand's indigenous character. It is always easier for the public to focus attention upon the more attractive or endangered species – the beautiful wattlebirds, dense lowland podocarp forest, or the rare and colourful tree brooms (species of *Notospartium* and *Chordospartium*) of Marlborough. But should we not also be concerned about the eclipse of the sandbinding sedge, pingao? Its curved shiny golden leaves not only bring a warmth to our seascapes but they are also valued by Maoris for weaving and the making of decorative wall panels (*tukutuku*). Or the jointed-rush *Sporadanthus*, an endangered endemic genus once so common in the peatlands of the Auckland–Waikato district. Now, like the tussock grasslands of the South Island, these wetlands are inexorably losing their indigenous character. And what interest is there in the protection of those fascinating but somewhat frightening creatures – the giant wetas (species of *Deinacrida*)? To the Maori people, the species of giant weta on Little Barrier Island was known as *weta-punga* (*punga* was a god who ruled over deformed and ugly creatures), and Europeans have probably also constructed myths about these gentle 'dinosaurs of the insect world'. Apart from a small relict population near Te Kuiti, the three species of giant weta have been banished by predators to offshore islands – Little Barrier, the Poor Knights and some of the Cook Strait Islands such as Mana Island. How many trout fishermen are aware of our diverse fauna of native freshwater fish – the lamprey, bullies, mudfish and the 10 species of Galaxiidae? Some of them may be as ancient as many of the more notable species in our terrestrial fauna. But we know so little of them and their shy and secretive ways that we tend to overlook the devastating effect of forest clearance and wetland drainage on their habitat, and the introduction of trout upon their numbers. The damage that introduced mammals such as stoats, possums and deer do to our forests and alpine biota is all too visible, and there is a longstanding policy of eradicating these animals. No such regulation exists to control the increasing populations of exotic fish in our rivers, and the decimation of our native freshwater fish continues largely unseen and easily forgotten. Future generations may be lucky to taste whitebait, let alone ever see a giant kokopu or greyling in our rivers.

REDFINNED BULLY
The redfinned bully, Gobiomorphus huttonii, *is one of the commonest and most widespread of New Zealand's freshwater fishes, yet the colourful male shown here (about 10 cm in length) is virtually unknown to the general public. All six species of bullys are endemic but are related to similar small freshwater fishes with marine tolerances found in tropical Asia and the Pacific.*

OUR PRICELESS HERITAGE: The islands of New Zealand are a remarkable biological storehouse, with so much of the biota having an ancestry on the supercontinent of Gondwanaland 200 to 150 million years ago. Yet much of this antiquity has been lost by the phenomenal changes to the land that have occurred in the last 150 years – a miniscule fragment of geological history compared with the hundreds of millions of years of evolution that preceded man's arrival in these ancient islands. What is left today is only a tattered remnant of the biological mantle of primitive New Zealand, but it is a heritage we cannot afford to lose.

PRIMAEVAL FOREST
Most indigenous forest has now been modified by the elimination of ground-cover and subcanopy plants which are palatable to wild introduced animals such as deer and goats. Here, on inaccessible Table Mountain in Coromandel State Forest Park, the condition of the forest interior is still similar to that found in primaeval New Zealand.

CHAPTER TWO

Island Sanctuaries

Today the New Zealand biological region, stretching from the subtropical Kermadec Islands in the north to subantarctic Campbell Island in the south, includes over 660 islands. But it was not always so. The land mass that separated from the rest of Gondwanaland was gradually worn down to an archipelago of islands, which slowly altered in size and shape over the following millennia. Then, with the onset of the Pleistocene Ice Ages (2 million years ago), the sea receded dramatically all over the world, as much of the land was covered with glaciers and ice sheets. At the height of the last glacial period, some 17,000 to 14,000 years ago, the three main islands of New Zealand and many of the smaller ones formed one large island or land mass. Islands close to New Zealand were, however, connected and disconnected again several times during the Pleistocene, as the sea level fluctuated with changes in temperature. When the glaciations ended around 10,000 years ago, the sea level finally rose, leaving the islands of New Zealand roughly as they are today.

The oceanic environment dominates the ecology of all these islands. Climates tend to be milder than on the adjacent mainland, although wind batters the exposed islands of Cook Strait and the Southern Ocean. Only plants capable of withstanding wind-borne salt can survive. Soils are usually similar to those on the mainland; some are exceptionally fertile, because of the activity of seabirds in cycling nitrogen, potassium and phosphorus from the ocean ecosystem.

The great majority of our islands (about 630) lie within 50 km of the mainland. They are termed 'offshore' islands and would all have been connected during the last glacial period. The other 30 are 'outlying' islands (more than 50 km from the mainland) such as the Kermadec, Three Kings, Chatham, Snares, Bounty, Antipodes, Auckland and Campbell Islands, which have been isolated from the mainland for a long time. The vegetation of the offshore islands is generally similar to that of the adjacent coast, with the exception of the Poor Knights Islands which have several endemic species; outlying islands, however, tend to show a high degree of endemism in their plant and animal life because of their isolation. While isolation from the mainland has influenced the ecology of our islands, so too has latitude. Therefore, the islands around New Zealand can be usefully discussed in six regional groupings: the subtropical outlying islands; the northern offshore islands; the islands of Cook Strait and the Marlborough Sounds; the southern offshore islands; the Chatham Islands; and the subantarctic islands.

◁ LONG ISLAND
Long Island in the Marlborough Sounds, is just one of the scores of islands that have been formed in this landscape of drowned valleys.

A RARE SPECIES
The very rare woody climber, Tecomanthe speciosa, *is the only New Zealand member of the tropical Bignonia family. It is one of 13 plants endemic to the Three Kings Islands, 50 km off Cape Reinga.*

SUBTROPICAL, OUTLYING ISLANDS: The Kermadec Islands are a volcanic group 1,000 km north-east of Auckland and have probably been isolated since their formation. The largest island, Raoul Island, is still an active volcano. As on other volcanic islands of the Pacific region, the lava flows are colonised at an early stage by *Metrosideros* forest, in this case the Kermadec pohutukawa. The Kermadec group contains 21 endemic plant species or subspecies, and five endemic subspecies of birds, but the islands have been severely modified by fires and introduced goats, cats and rats. This transformation of the original ecosystem is nowhere more evident than on Macauley Island in the group, where the action of fire and goats has turned all the 300 hectares into a short grassland.

The Three Kings Islands, about 50 km north-west of Cape Reinga, also have a subtropical climate. In the biota are some unusual relict forms which may never have reached the New Zealand mainland. There are 13 endemic plants on the island including the rare woody climber *Tecomanthe speciosa*. There is also a high degree of endemism in the invertebrate fauna, which includes 25 different land snails found only in the group. Like the Kermadecs, the Three Kings have suffered seriously from goats, but these were eliminated in 1946 and the vegetation is now recovering.

NORTHERN ISLANDS: The inner islands of the Hauraki Gulf Maritime Park, such as Rangitoto, Kawau and Motuihe, are among the most attractive in New Zealand. The climate is warm and humid, with frost-free winters. Three of these northern islands (Mayor, Rangitoto and White Islands) have shown recent volcanic activity. (See Chapter 9.) Virtually all the northern islands have a long history of Maori occupation and European attempts at settlement. Now that pigs or goats have been eliminated from many of these modified islands, such as Aorangi (Poor Knights group) and Cuvier Island off the Coromandel Peninsula, the vegetation is recovering. The Poor Knights, Hen and Chickens and Aldermen Islands are all biologically significant, but probably the most important northern island is Little Barrier Island, which is a sanctuary for many rare forest birds and which carries some of the finest lowland forest remaining north of the South Island.

SHORE PLOVER
The shore plover, Thinornis novaeseelandiae, *is one of New Zealand's rarest birds, now extinct on the main islands although it was fairly plentiful in the 1880s. It is confined now to tiny South East Island in the Chathams group.*

COOK STRAIT/MARLBOROUGH SOUNDS ISLANDS: North-westerly gales often lash these offshore islands. Instead of pohutukawa, the salt-resistant ngaio and shrubby taupata line the coast, along with other coastal trees typical of the Wellington region – kohekohe, karaka and akiraho (*Olearia paniculata*). The vegetation of virtually all of these islands has been modified by fire and grazing animals. The bird sanctuary, Kapiti Island, is the best known in the group, and although Norway rats, kiore and possums are present, cats, mustelids (such as stoats) and ship rats are fortunately absent. The relationship between tuatara and the large numbers of breeding seabirds (such as diving petrels and fairy prions) on some of these islands is also interesting: both often share the same burrow, even though tuatara prey upon the eggs and young birds.

SOUTHERN OFFSHORE ISLANDS: Resolution Island and Secretary Island are large islands that really form part of Fiordland. But both have had a significant role to play in conservation. For 15 dedicated, and finally fruitless, years from 1894, Richard Henry the government 'Curator and Caretaker of Resolution Island' laboured in vain to save kakapo and kiwi from marauding stoats and other predators by ferrying them from the mainland to Resolution Island. Sadly, the stoats followed him to prey upon his 'poor, simple, defenceless and flightless old New Zealanders'. Until 1967 Secretary Island was an excellent unmodified sequence of Fiordland vegetation, from sea level to subalpine grassland at 1,200 m. But just as stoats earlier swam to Resolution Island, deer have now invaded Secretary Island by swimming the 1-2 km of fiord separating it from the mainland, and are selectively browsing the vegetation.

The southern islands in Foveaux Strait and around Stewart Island are often simply called 'the mutton-bird islands' in reference to the legal harvesting of their population of sooty shearwater (*Puffinus griseus*) by the Rakiura Maoris. The rich birdlife of these southern islands has been severely depleted by rats and cats. However, these introduced animals are not the only predators upon petrels. Stewart Island wekas, introduced to offshore islands such as Codfish Island, have had a devastating impact, particularly on mottled petrels and the rare Cook's petrel. Consequently, they are being transferred back to Stewart Island where, ironically, they are now rare.

THE CHATHAM ISLANDS: This group, lying 900 km east of Christchurch, consists of four main islands, whose climate is windy, cloudy and cool. All the islands in the group have suffered severe losses through human settlement and the introduction of predators. The Chathams were settled by the first Polynesian voyagers and, in the intervening 1,000 years, much of their fauna has become extinct. Apart from the Three Kings Islands, no other part of New Zealand shows such a high degree of endemism, in both flora and fauna. Nearly half of the 33 woody plants are endemic to the islands. Fossil bones show that there were once giant rails, two snipes and a kakapo as well as a wide variety of interesting lagoon and forest birds. Three islands in the group, Rangatira (South East) Island and the two Mangere Islands, have been acquired as nature reserves, but there are still no nature reserves on the main Chatham Island.

SUBANTARCTIC ISLANDS: The Auckland, Antipodes, Bounty, Snares and Campbell Islands are bleak, cold islands set in the midst of the vast Southern Ocean. They all share persistent westerly winds, cold temperatures and overcast skies. Peat soils blanket the landscape, and the vegetation is mainly subalpine – grasslands (*Chionochloa antarctica* and *Poa* species), *Dracophyllum* scrub, alpine fellfields and bog communities. The podocarps and beech of the mainland are absent, but there are affinities with much of the flora of both New Zealand and southern Chile. There is also a high degree of endemism in the flora, and an ancient element that may perhaps represent a link with pre-glacial Antarctica. (See Chapter 8.) Some of the bog and fellfield plants are spectacular and colourful, compared with their mainland relatives. Why there are so many brightly flowered plants on the Auckland Islands – such as the purple and brown *Pleurophyllum*, the reddish-mauve *Anisotome antipoda* and the blue *Hebe benthamii* – is something of an enigma.

ISLANDS AS SANCTUARIES: Many of these islands now contain the last remnants of some of New Zealand's ancient flora and fauna. Human occupation has eliminated habitats and plant communities from the mainland through forest clearance, fire and agricultural development of wetlands; introduced animals have brought disease, predation or competition, so that many birds, reptiles and invertebrates are now confined to, or only breed on, these islands. To a large extent the islands are precious sanctuaries, 'living museums' protecting much of the biological richness of ancient Gondwanaland. Without our offshore islands we would probably no longer have the tuatara or Duvaucel's gecko, the stitchbird or the saddleback. With a few notable exceptions such as the gannet, black petrel and the royal albatross, most of our seabirds now nest on islands. Six of our 22 species of skink are confined to islands and the rarest of our three native frog species (all of ancient origin), Hamilton's frog, is found only in very restricted habitats on two small islands – Stephens Island in Cook Strait and Maud Island in the Marlborough Sounds.

EUROPEAN STOAT
The stoat, Mustela ermina, *along with the ferret and weasel, was brought into New Zealand in the 1880s to control rabbits. Instead, the stoat has shown a preference for rodents and small native birds. It is just one of the many introduced species to turn into an 'ecological disaster' for the native fauna.*

As many as 150 of our offshore and outlying islands are important refuges for indigenous species because of the absence of cats, mustelids, and Norway and ship rats. The impact of cats and rats on the native fauna can be illustrated by three historical examples: cats on Little Barrier and Stephens Islands and ship rats on Big South Cape Island off the south-western tip of Stewart Island. Cats probably reached Little Barrier Island by 1870 and their numbers built up rapidly. By the mid-1880s forest birds such as the saddleback had probably been exterminated and the numbers of stitchbirds and parakeets were very low. A major cat eradication programme was mounted in 1977, and by 1980 the population of cats (estimated to be as high as 800 in 1975) had been exterminated. Through this outstanding wildlife conservation effort, the robin, parakeet and stitchbird populations have now all increased markedly.

On Stephens Island cats were introduced after the lighthouse was built in 1894; at the same time most of the low forest of kohekohe and large-leaved milk tree was cleared. Four rare birds on the island were lost – the saddleback, kokako, the New Zealand thrush and the Stephens Island wren. It is a tragic story, for on such a small island cats could have been eradicated earlier – or simply not introduced. Somehow, Hamilton's frog, one of the rarest frogs in the world, managed to hang on under its small boulderbank near the summit of the island, even though this habitat had been denuded of forest through sheep and cattle grazing.

The most recent and dramatic loss to New Zealand's fauna occurred through an irruption of ship rats on Big South Cape Island in the early 1960s. The island had been free of rodents, including kiore, and there was enough food to sustain a high population of ship rats for at least three years. In this brief period, four rare birds (Stewart Island snipe, Stead's bush wren, Stewart Island robin and Stewart Island fernbird) and the Stewart Island short-tailed bat disappeared.

A few outlying islands are still in a pristine condition today because of the complete absence of introduced predators. This important group includes the Meyer Islands in the Kermadec group, Adams and Disappointment Islands in the Aucklands group, the Snares, and Bounty Islands. The rarely visited Antipodes Islands are also largely unmodified since the only surviving introduced mammal, the mouse, does not appear to be having any significant effect on bird populations.

Despite the long list of species that have been lost from our islands, or are in danger of extinction, island sanctuaries do offer hope of survival through the transfer of breeding populations. The saddleback, for example, has been successfully reintroduced to Cuvier Island, and, in one of the most remarkable stories of conservation, the entire Chatham Island black robin population of seven birds was moved from their dying forest habitat on the summit plateau of Little Mangere Island to a new regenerating forest habitat on Mangere Island. Less well known are the efforts to save the little spotted kiwi: the almost chance transfer of birds to Kapiti Island earlier this century, and the more recent attempt to shift the last pair of the former D'Urville Island population to Maud Island in the Marlborough Sounds. Maud Island has been the foster home for the survivors of another drama – the intensive effort to save the remaining flightless parrots, kakapo, from their last stand against predators in Fiordland and Stewart Island.

TARANGA ISLAND, HAURAKI GULF
Taranga Island is the largest of the Hen and Chickens group, the islands that have been so important in the fight for survival of one of New Zealand's rare wattlebirds. The saddleback (*Philesturnus carunculatus*) was originally found in forests throughout the North and South Islands and surrounding islands, but its population declined dramatically around the 1890s. The North Island saddleback was known to survive only on Taranga Island, until in 1964 the Wildlife Service moved birds to other islands in the group where they have bred successfully. The South Island saddleback also only survived on some of the South Cape Islands off the southern tip of Stewart Island, until birds were again transferred to other islands for breeding.
▽

PIED SHAGS, *Phalacrocorax v. varius*

Pied shags inhabit estuaries and harbours around our coasts and offshore islands. They prefer the warmer north, but are found further south as far as Stewart Island. Pied shags usually roost and nest high in overhanging trees; on Little Barrier Island the colonies are in pohutukawa trees clustered along the tops of coastal cliffs, while on Stewart Island they are found in a close relative of the pohutukawa, the southern rata, along tidal rivers. Perched on rocks or branches with their wings spread out to dry, shags are a familiar sight around our coast.

LITTLE BARRIER, NORTH-EAST COAST
Behind the boulder beaches of Little Barrier, the land rises steeply, forming cliffs in many places. This remote area is Hingaia ('fallen'), where a massive slip has formed an area known as Pohutukawa Flat. Here, the forest canopy consists of widely spreading, open-headed pohutukawa trees. Elsewhere, the coastal forest is a mixture of hardwoods like taraire, tawa, karaka and kohekohe, with nikau palms adding a subtropical note to the landscape.

△
PYRROSIA FERN
The thick-leafed fern *Pyrrosia serpens* thrives in sunny open places. This is a typical habitat on a Little Barrier Island boulderbank, where it shares the space with mosses, lichens and tangles of *Muehlenbeckia complexa*.

SUMMIT RIDGES, LITTLE BARRIER ▷
For a small island, Little Barrier is remarkably rugged. Although some of the lower slopes were once milled and farmed, these high ridges remain untouched. In the foreground the large neinei (*Dracophyllum traversii*) mingles with flax and the sedge, *Gahnia*. It is on these ridges that the migratory Cook's petrels breed.

COOK'S PETREL, *Pterodoma c. cooki*
Cook's petrel is an ocean bird, migrating across the Pacific to the coasts of North and South America. Like most petrels, it breeds in burrows dug out of the ground; but the Cook's petrel and black petrel are unusual in making their burrows at least 300 m above sea-level. They were formerly found nesting in the mainland ranges, but few have been seen there in recent years. These delicate little seabirds are vulnerable on land, and easily fall prey to cats, wekas and rats.

◁ AWAROA STREAM, LITTLE BARRIER
Fresh-water habitats are not common on our offshore islands. Most streams are short and steep-sided. Here, only metres from the boulder beach, Awaroa stream broadens under dense coastal forest.

◁ BROOM, *Carmichaelia williamsii*
This large broom now grows principally on the Poor Knights, Little Barrier and Aldermen Islands, and Sail Rock (Hen and Chickens group). Its habitat has been greatly reduced by land development and grazing, and only a few patches remain on the mainland.

BLACK PETREL, *Procellaria parkinsoni* ▷
Another, larger member of the petrel family, the black petrel, also breeds on the high ridges of Little and Great Barrier Islands. This adult was returning to feed a plump down-covered chick. It landed heavily through a dense canopy of foliage only 2 m from its burrow on a very dark night.

CHATHAM ISLAND FORGET-ME-NOT, *Myosotidium hortensia*
This magnificent forget-me-not is found in its natural state only on the Chatham Islands, although it is now a popular garden plant throughout New Zealand. On a single plant up to a metre wide, the big flower heads rise out of a nest of shiny dark green leaves. An outstanding feature of the Chathams is the large number of endemic plant species – nowhere is the need for reserves more urgent.

Previous page
BOULDER BEACH, LITTLE BARRIER
This famous pohutukawa grove hugs the headland beyond a seemingly endless stretch of boulders.

CHATHAM ISLAND ICE PLANT, *Disphyma papillatum*
This bright little ice plant is also confined to the Chatham Islands. Another plant found only on these islands is the beautiful Chatham Island daisy, *Olearia semidentata*, whose mauve flowers brighten the moors of the southern tablelands of the main Chatham Island. Why so many colourful plants are restricted to outlying islands such as the Chathams and the subantarctic Auckland Islands has long been a matter of scientific speculation.

△ HOKATAKA, *Corokia macrocarpa*
Another garden plant, hokataka, is a handsome shrub, usually about 2 m tall. It too is found naturally only on Chatham Island, where it inhabits the forest and forest margins.

◁ *Euphorbia glauca*
This milk weed, our only member of the genus *Euphorbia* was once common among the sands and rocks around the coastline. It has now been eliminated from many areas, and survives best on offshore islands.

POHUTUKAWA FLAT,
LITTLE BARRIER

On Little Barrier Island the pohutukawa forest is relatively undisturbed and very dense because of the absence of browsing animals. The ground is sometimes carpeted with astelias, as in this photograph. ▽

CHATHAM ISLAND YELLOW-CROWNED PARAKEET, *Cyanoramphus auriceps forbesi*

Both the yellow-crowned parakeet and the red-crowned parakeet (*Cyanoramphus n. novaezelandiae*) were formerly common in forests throughout the country. The red-crowned parakeet is now rare on the mainland, and found mostly on offshore and outlying islands. The yellow-crowned parakeet is seen more frequently, particularly in large areas of forest. The subspecies from the Chatham Islands, Forbes parakeet, is now found only on Little Mangere in the Chathams group.

STITCHBIRD, *Notiomystis cincta* ▷

Female (*left*), male (*right*). Like other honeyeaters such as the tui and the bellbird, the stitchbird is particularly fond of nectar, and is drawn to trees such as rata, pohutukawa and rewarewa. But it feeds also on insects and fruit. The stitchbird was formerly widespread in the forests of the North Island and Great Barrier Island, but has been confined to Little Barrier Island since about 1885. Even here it has, until recently, been threatened by wild cats.

HAMILTON'S FROG, ▷
Leiopelma hamiltoni
Hamilton's frog is the rarest of New Zealand's three native species of frog, all members of the ancient genus *Leiopelma.* This tiny frog is restricted to Stephens Island in Cook Strait and Maud Island in the Marlborough Sounds – both quite devoid of any permanent water! On Stephens Island it lives under a boulderbank on the summit, safe from tuataras and burrow-nesting seabirds.

KIORE, *Rattus exulans*
Kiore, the Polynesian rat, was introduced to New Zealand by Polynesian voyagers to whom it was a choice item of diet. Once considered to be mainly vegetarian, the kiore is now thought to prey on young birds and reptiles. When Europeans introduced the Norway and ship rats, they proved too fierce a competition for the kiore, which was eventually eliminated from the main islands; today it is only found on certain offshore and outlying islands. It is the smallest of the three rats found in the New Zealand region and a native of South East Asia.
▽

DUVAUCEL'S GECKO, ▷
Hoplodactylus duvauceli
New Zealand's largest gecko is found in a few coastal areas and rat-free islands, like some of the Trio and Brothers Islands in Cook Strait. It is nocturnal, emerging at night to climb trees, where it eats insects and nectar.

CHAPTER THREE

Coastal Margins

The main islands of New Zealand are elongated and sinuous. No part of the land is more than 130 km from the sea, and only in the intermontane basins of Central Otago and the upper Waitaki is the climatic influence of the surrounding oceans diminished. The coastline of about 10,000 km is very long for a land mass of 27 million hectares. And it is a coastline marked by amazing diversity: the rocky headlands and surf beaches of the wild coastline fronting the Waitakere Ranges on Auckland's west coast; the sandy beaches and dunes of Ninety Mile Beach and the Hokianga, the Manawatu or Golden Bay in Nelson; the huge gravel and sand curve of Farewell Spit; the deeply land-locked harbours of Banks and Otago Peninsulas where the sea has breached ancient volcanoes. Some of the most dramatic coastal landforms are in Fiordland – the magnificent fiords formed when the sea flooded mountain valleys as the glaciers retreated – and in the Marlborough Sounds, the valleys that have been drowned as the north-eastern tip of the South Island gradually downwarps into Cook Strait. Just across Cook Strait, the southern tip of the Rimutaka Range is progressively rising out of the sea. Here, at Turakirae Head, a series of boulder beaches indicates at least four major uplifts during the past 5,000 years.

These different coastal landforms have evolved over the last 14,000 years since the post-glacial sea level began to rise. Some sections of hard rock coastline are highly resistant to wave action and coastal currents, and can be considered as corner-stones – in particular, North Cape, Cape Runaway, Coromandel Peninsula and Wellington in the North Island and the Marlborough Sounds, the coast of Abel Tasman National Park, Heaphy Bluff, Fiordland, the Catlins coast, and Banks and Otago Peninsulas in the South Island. In between, the coastline is simpler, with sand and other erosional debris tending to fill in bays, form spits and generally smooth out the coastline.

◁ HAURAKI GULF
A dead pohutukawa tree is silhouetted against the morning sky on the coast of the Hauraki Gulf.

ROCKY COASTLINE, WAIWERA
Some of the many different landforms along our coast – wave-cut platforms in the Hauraki Gulf.

OCEANS AND COASTAL WATERS: Like the land itself, the oceans around New Zealand contain a range of habitats. There are deep-sea basins and canyons such as the Hikurangi and Kermadec Trenches; there is an extensive area of 'continental shelf', roughly equivalent to the land area of New Zealand, lying between shoreline and 180 m depth. These underwater features deflect the dominant West Wind Drift (the oceanic current driven from west to east below Tasmania by the winds of the 'Roaring Forties') into local coastal currents around New Zealand. Consequently, the western shores of New Zealand, in particular, have been open to colonisation by organisms which 'ride the West Wind Drift'. For instance, many shallow-water marine animals, such as some starfish, show a circum-polar distribution consistent with dispersal on the West Wind Drift. Many other creatures – from the monarch butterfly to the white-faced heron – have been blown to our coasts from Australia and subsequently bred here.

There are about 400 different marine fish in the waters around New Zealand, that is, above the broad sea-floor extending from the Three Kings Islands in the north to Campbell Island in the subantarctic. Unlike New Zealand's terrestrial flora and fauna, this fish fauna is capable of crossing wide oceans relatively easily. Any ancient distribution patterns are thus masked by present-day environmental conditions and fluctuating populations. Large marine mammals also migrate through New Zealand's waters; 32 species of whale have been recorded and three of the largest whales (sperm, right and humpback) regularly migrate here in spring and autumn; dolphins and porpoises are relatively common. Four species of seal, New Zealand fur seal, leopard seal, elephant seal and Hooker's sea lion, are normally resident in our waters, coming ashore to breed in the subantarctic islands, Stewart Island and the southern regions of the South Island. The fur seal also ranges as far north as Cook Strait.

The coastal waters above the continental shelf are the most productive of the marine habitats. Here nutrients are washed from the land and a warmer layer of water lies close to the surface, continually mixed by the wind and heat-induced convection currents. Other nutrients rise from the colder, deep sea. It is here in the near-surface layer that probably 90 per cent of marine organic matter is synthesised, by microscopic plants called phytoplankton which, like land plants, use the sun's energy to convert carbon dioxide into carbohydrates and other digestible chemical compounds. This is the first link in most marine food chains: the phytoplankton (usually algae) are grazed by zooplankton (animal plankton) and the pelagic fishes (those that inhabit these upper layers of the sea as distinct from fish which prefer the sea floor). At times an exploding population of oceanic plankton is driven into coastal waters and a spectacular feeding mêlée ensues. Predators such as trevally often herd this plankton to the surface, where they are joined by other small predators such as koheru and jack mackerel, which in turn may be preyed upon by kahawai and kingfish. Flocks of gulls, terns and even tiny diving petrels often join in the excitement of the feast.

VARIABLE OYSTERCATCHER
This oystercatcher, Haematopus unicolor, *is generally found looking for shellfish and worms on beaches and estuaries. It is larger than the South Island pied oystercatcher (p. 127), with which it is easily confused because it has a 'pied' as well as a 'pure black' phase.*

THE INTERTIDAL ZONE: The shore between high and low water is subject to constantly changing conditions. Within this narrow zone there is an almost bewildering variety of plant and animal life. This diversity is greatest on rocky shores where the exposed rocks provide a firm anchor for seaweeds, many of them quite colourful. Some, like the brown and red algae, extend from low tide level out to a depth of up to 30 m in the coastal waters. By contrast, sandy shores foster little marine plant life; the beach at any one time is a 'river of sand' formed by the movement of millions of grains of sand and marine debris.

The species of seaweed in the rocky intertidal zone vary according to latitude and the degree of exposure to wave action. In the colder waters of southern New Zealand, for instance, the huge kelp 'forests' growing at the base of the intertidal zone will usually be giant kelp (*Macrocystis*), which can extend up to 50 m in length, while the smaller kelps, *Lessonia variegata* and *Ecklonia radiata*, are more common in central and northern waters. On very exposed, rocky coasts the tough, dark-brown bull kelps (*Durvillea*), anchor themselves to the rocks by means of a stress-resisting holdfast. In shallow, more sheltered areas of rocky coast, the bladder kelps (*Carpophyllum*) can form dense tangled jungles that defy even the most determined of divers.

Marine animals on rocky or sandy shores likewise reflect the effects of latitude and exposure. In northern New Zealand, rocks in the middle part of the intertidal zone are usually encrusted with rock oysters; around Wellington and the Marlborough Sounds, the blue mussel generally occupies this niche. Sandy beach dwellers – crabs, toheroa, pipi and cockles – are also influenced by subtle environmental differences in their choice of habitat. Some prefer coarse sand on open beaches; others, such as bivalves and worms, like the finer sands and muds of estuaries.

Unlike the algae that have so profusely colonised the waters of rocky shores, few higher plants are able to survive submerged in sea water. Only the eelgrasses (*Zostera*) can grow wholly in this intertidal zone, although a number of others – such as mangroves, glasswort, and the sedge and rush communities of salt marshes – can withstand inundation for short periods in each tidal cycle. *Zostera* can be thought of as a pioneer plant stabilising a range of sandy and silty flats. Green 'fields' or beds of *Zostera* are characteristic of the Manukau Harbour with its narrow fringe of mangroves (*Avicennia resinifera*). Where the mangrove thrives further north in the Kaipara Harbour, the Bay of Islands and the Hauraki Gulf, it brings a subtropical element to the seascape. The mangrove is to maritime Auckland what coastal flax (*Phormium cookianum*) and taupata are to the wind-blasted, rocky coastline of Wellington.

The animal life of *Zostera* fields, salt marshes and mangrove shrubland is particularly rich. Flounder and mullet abound in *Zostera* fields with their organic-rich muds and high populations of gastropods (limpets and sea snails) and crustaceans (crabs and shrimps); the mud among the mangroves teems with crabs, molluscs and worms with barnacles and rock oysters clinging to the roots and trunk of the shrubs. Small wonder then that birdlife is so profuse in these northern estuaries – the Manukau, Tauranga and Kaipara, the Firth of Thames, and Parengarenga in the far north. Here the northern oystercatchers move purposefully across the sand and mudflats at the estuary mouth while large formations of pied stilt systematically probe the mud with their slender bills. The banded dotterel is an amusing inhabitant of the sandy beaches: superbly camouflaged, he nevertheless persists in an agitated feigning of injury when disturbed. Many other inhabitants of these estuaries are migratory Arctic-breeding birds, such as the godwit, golden plover and knot, which 'winter-over' here during our summer. The different flocks restlessly parading these estuarine feeding grounds seem to present a bewildering chaos of noise and colour, yet there is an unseen web of feeding and behavioural relationships among them all. Some groups intermingle while feeding on the mudflats; some are fiercely territorial; some, like the aptly named turnstone, specialise in the outer limits of the estuary, overturning stones to find crabs and worms.

ABOVE THE TIDE: Sandy beaches which are so popular for recreation are perhaps the best known of our natural landscapes. Yet few people appreciate that the marram grass and woolly-tufted harestail fixing the foredune are introduced plants which have largely replaced the native sandbinders, *Spinifex* and the golden-coloured endemic sedge, pingao (*Desmoschoenus spiralis*). It is indeed now a rare sight to see an unmodified pingao/spinifex dune on the main islands outside of North Cape. Behind the foredune a more complex, continuous cover of plants, both native (*Coprosma*, *Cassinia* and *Pimelea*) and introduced (lupins), stabilises the raw sand. Gradually organic matter accumulates in the sand, slowly transforming it into a soil with enough water-holding capacity for other shrubs, and ultimately coastal forest, to establish.

One of the most outstanding examples of a sequence of sand country landscapes is to be found in the Manawatu. During the closing stages of the last glaciation (10,000-20,000 years ago), the oldest dunes (Koputaroa phase) were formed about 20 km inland from the present coastline at Himatangi. Three subsequent phases of sand dunes were built up as the coastline moved westwards – Foxton (2,000-3,000 years ago), Motuiti (500-750 years ago) and the current Waitarere foredune system (about 75 years ago). Behind the foredunes, the sand country landscape presents an amazing sight from the air: a phalanx of long dunes, all arrayed with military precision, seems to march from Levin to Wanganui in parallel columns oriented to the prevailing north-westerly wind. With increasing age these sand dune phases show progressive development of soil organic matter and vegetation. On the drier intermediate dune phases, bracken fern (*Pteridium*), tutu (*Coriaria*) and kanuka were the main species; on the old dune phases a forest of matai, pukatea, kahikatea and tawa became established, with totara, titoki and kanuka predominating on the drier sites. These landforms have now been developed almost completely into pasture and pine forest. The remnants of this remarkable sequence of sand country native vegetation are so minute that travellers can only imagine what the original landscape must have looked like.

MANGROVES
Mangroves, Avicennia resinifera, *are among the few woody plants that have evolved ways of living on the margins of estuaries.*

On rocky beaches a variety of plants is found, often in quite distinct zones. Succulence is a common adaptation, seen in the iceplants and the common glasswort (*Sarcocornia quinqueflora*). Different species of turf plants, grasses and ferns replace the sandbinders of the dunes. The black shore skink (*Leiolepisma suteri*) can be glimpsed here on the warmer, northern coast, but several other skinks and the widespread gecko, *Hoplodactylus maculatus*, also prey on insects and spiders in this zone.

The coastal forest is distinguished by different trees at different latitudes. Pohutukawa and karaka often line the warmer, northern coasts. Here, too, the nikau palm (*Rhopalostylis sapida*) once thrived. Dense nikau groves still remain in some places, like the coastline north of Karamea where Heaphy Track walkers can spend a day passing through one of the most distinctive forests along our coastline. Ngaio (*Myoporum laetum*), and the shiny-leaved taupata characterise the Wellington area and southern rata (*Metrosideros umbellata*) adds a blaze of brilliant red flowers where it descends to sea level on the Catlins coast and Stewart Island.

MARINE RESERVES: Although 10 per cent (2.7 million hectares) of New Zealand's land area is protected as national parks and reserves, only 3,000 hectares of coast and sea have been given equivalent protection in two marine reserves on the east coast of Northland (Goat Island/Cape Rodney and the Poor Knights Islands). Perhaps the sea is still considered as our 'last frontier', for the shameless exploitation of marine resources such as the Chatham Island crayfish and the Golden Bay scallops in recent years has all the hallmarks of the gold-rushes of the nineteenth century.

New Zealand has, however, benefited from a wide variety of terrestrial reserves involving coastal land. Virtually all our important offshore islands are nature reserves and coastal reserves have been grouped into maritime parks in the Hauraki Gulf, Bay of Islands and Marlborough Sounds. In addition, three national parks – Fiordland, Westland and Abel Tasman – fortunately protect some of the most scenic coastline of the South Island.

SOUTHERN BLACK-BACKED GULLS, *Larus dominicanus*
The southern black-backed gull (karoro) is the largest of the three New Zealand gulls, and is one of the few native birds to have increased in number since the Europeans arrived. Settlement has reduced the gulls' coastal feeding grounds only slightly, and they now find ample food scavenging in towns and on farmland.

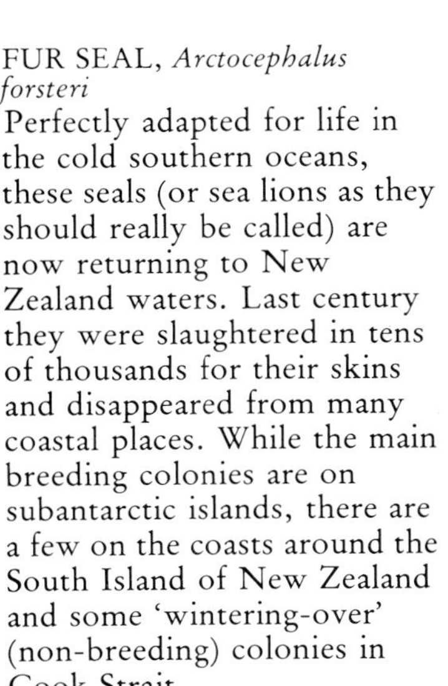

FUR SEAL, *Arctocephalus forsteri*
Perfectly adapted for life in the cold southern oceans, these seals (or sea lions as they should really be called) are now returning to New Zealand waters. Last century they were slaughtered in tens of thousands for their skins and disappeared from many coastal places. While the main breeding colonies are on subantarctic islands, there are a few on the coasts around the South Island of New Zealand and some 'wintering-over' (non-breeding) colonies in Cook Strait.

BLUE PENGUIN, *Eudyptula minor*
Several species of penguin are to be found in New Zealand waters, but most are found only on the southern coast or in the subantarctic. Subspecies of the blue penguin, however, are found on all parts of our coast, from Stewart Island to North Cape. They nest in natural hollows or in burrows that they take over from petrels. Standing at about 40 cm, they are the smallest of our penguins; they move awkwardly over the ground but are fast-moving in the water.

KAREKARE: AUCKLAND'S WILD WEST COAST
Ocean swells from the Tasman Sea crash in against the cliffs at Karekare. The forces of nature on New Zealand's exposed coasts are uncompromising, and only well-adapted species, like the bull kelp in this picture, can survive long. The sandy beaches linking rocky headlands become the sea's rubbish dump, collecting debris as various as logs, seaweed, and this dead fish.

BULL KELP, *Durvillea antarctica*
The intertidal zone is rich in both plant and animal life. Kelp forests often line the lower edges of the zone on rocky coasts, but the type of kelp varies from region to region. The tough bull kelp is characteristic of the colder, southern coast, but it grows also in many exposed, rocky spots further north. With its unusually strong holdfast, it is well adapted to withstand storms and constant wave action.

FLOTSAM
Seaweed (*Macrocystis pyrifera*), strung like washing between two rocks, is dried by wind and sun.
▽

WHITE-FRONTED TERN,
Sterna striata
The forked tail of this delicate little seabird has led to the name 'sea swallow'. It is the commonest of the three terns found frequently in the New Zealand region. Like the much bigger Caspian tern (*Hydroprogne caspia*), it frequents the coast, while the black-fronted tern (*Sterna albostriata*) inhabits inland rivers and estuaries. The white-fronted tern breeds only in the New Zealand region, in shallow hollows along the sand dunes or on rocky faces. Its breeding colonies are sometimes found in association with colonies of red-billed and black-backed gulls, and on occasion with black-fronted terns.

COASTAL VEGETATION
Salt and wind constantly shape the coastal vegetation and limit what can grow. These remnants of a karaka grove have been battered and bent by sea winds, while on the ground shrubs of *Muehlenbeckia complexa* have evolved a prostrate form in order to survive.

REEF HERON, *Egretta s. sacra*
The reef heron faces strong competition from the newer arrival, the white-faced heron (*Ardea novaehollandiae*), and has declined in numbers recently. Unlike the latter species, the reef heron nests in pairs in shallow caves, rather than in trees. It is a coastal bird, feeding primarily on fish caught in tidal waters.

Top left
SNAPPER SCALES

Top right
WATER, SAND AND SUNSET

Above
COCKLE BANK

Right
COASTAL BUBBLES

Far right
PAUA SHELL

Opposite page
TIDAL SAND FINGERS

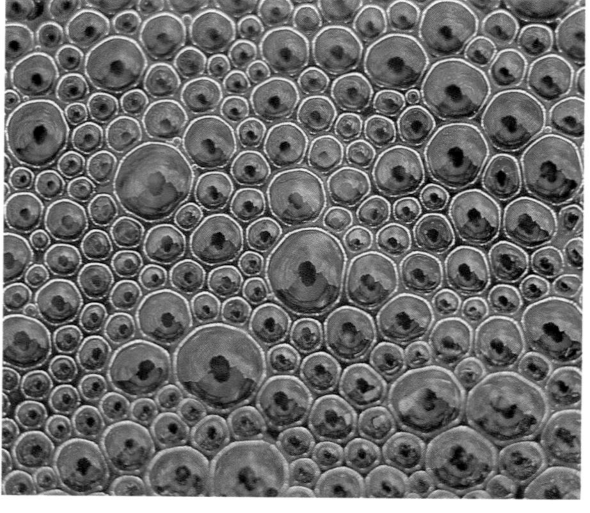

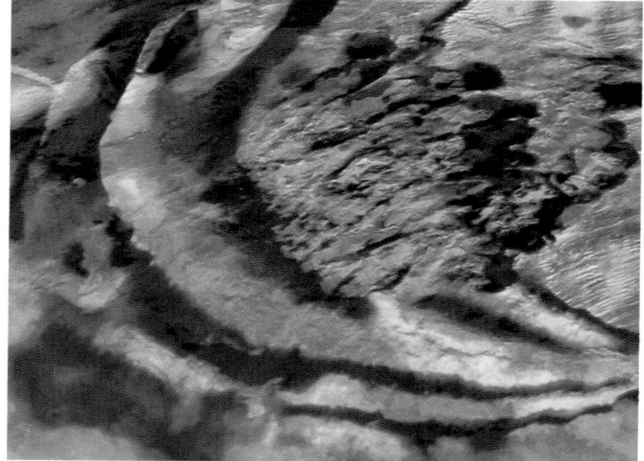

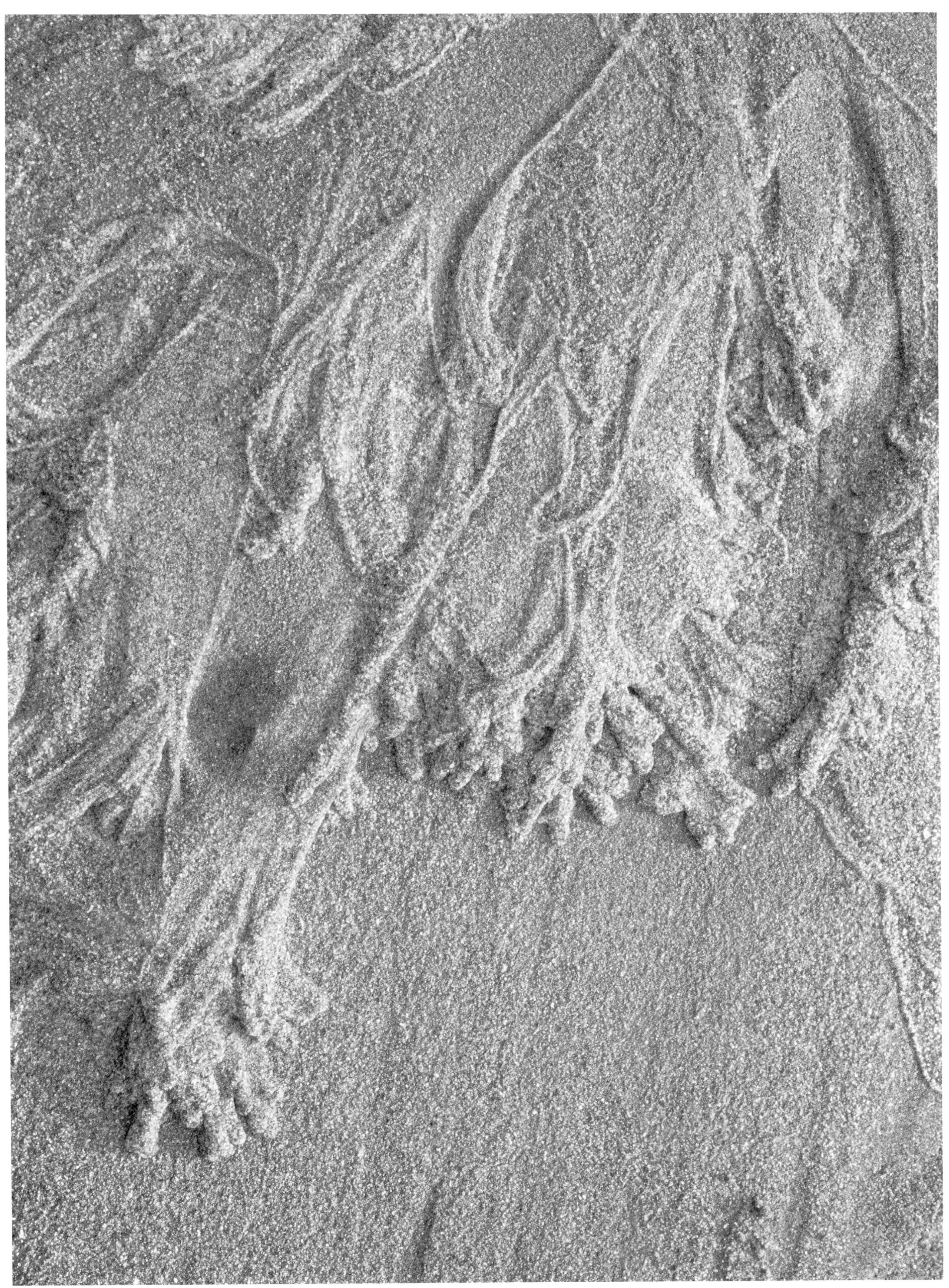

△
ICE PLANT, *Carpobrotus odulis*
This large succulent plant, which sports yellow or pink flowers, was introduced from South Africa and is now successfully established on our beaches. The endemic Maori ice plant, horokaka (*Disphyma australe*), is smaller and often forms attractive mats trailing over rocks and cliff faces.

SHINGLE BEACHES, COOK STRAIT
The gravels and sands of beaches are gradually colonised by tall grasses, such as tussocks of *Poa triodioides* and flat mats of coastal raoulia. Since this photograph was taken, lupin has spread over much of this area.

SAND HIBISCUS, *Hibiscus trionum* ▷
This hibiscus grows naturally only on the North Auckland peninsula and on Great Barrier and Mayor Islands. The two hibiscus species found in New Zealand may not be truly native.

△
HARESTAIL, *Lagurus ovatus*
The fluffy harestail, another introduced species, is probably children's favourite seaside grass.

◁ *Geranium molle*
Even the introduced weed, *Geranium molle*, can grow in the harsh coastal environment. Finding shelter among the much taller marram grasses, it brings a touch of colour to sand dunes.

SAND DUNES, TANGIMOANA
It is now almost impossible to find sand dunes covered only with indigenous plants. Native spinifex, pingao, coprosma and convolvulus (to name but a few) now have to compete with the introduced marram grass and lupins. All of these plants help bind the dunes and prevent wind erosion.

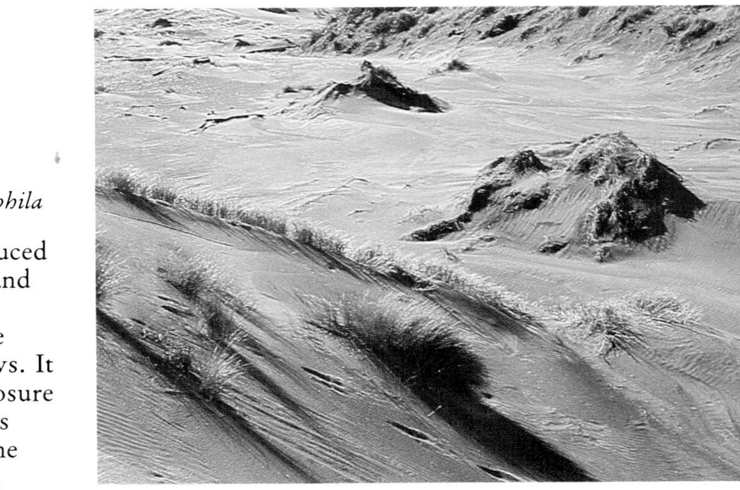

MARRAM GRASS, *Ammophila arenaria*
Marram grass was introduced to help stabilise coastal sand dune country. Its tough rhizomes help to bind the loose soil in which it grows. It can tolerate constant exposure to salt-laden winds, and is often the only plant on the dunes nearest the sea.
▽

◁ FIXED DUNES AND DEPRESSIONS
Behind the foredunes that face the sea, other plants less tolerant of salt and winds can establish themselves. This depression is several hundred metres from the beach, and there is enough moisture in the soil to allow the native jointed rush (*Leptocarpus similis*) and one of the introduced pampas grasses to grow. A plant of the native toetoe is seen top right.

RAOULIA
Raoulias are some of our hardiest plants. They are among the first to colonise certain open situations, such as beaches and river beds, from sea level up to alpine regions. In flower, their sweet perfume attracts many insects. Their compact, cushion-like shape and grey-white colour have earned some species the name 'vegetable sheep'.

DUNE PONDS, KAREKARE ▷
Shallow ponds form in the dunes where the water-table is close to the surface. They usually dry up during the summer heat, which kills off any plants that may have been encouraged to take root there. Here marram grass can still grow on the small mounds of sand.

Muehlenbeckia axillaris ▷
Three species of *Muehlenbeckia* provide food for the copper butterfly. This plant was photographed at Kairakau in Hawke's Bay, only 50 m from the ocean, yet the species is also found in gravelly places in montane, subalpine and grassland areas.

COMMON COPPER BUTTERFLY, *Lycaena salustius*
Although it mostly frequents the coast, this little butterfly is found almost anywhere in New Zealand. When basking it opens its wings far enough to absorb as much heat as it requires. Its eggs are laid on *Muehlenbeckia* leaves. This butterfly could be regarded as archaic, because it is a northern hemisphere type not found in Australia. But it is capable of good flight, and could therefore disperse across the oceans.
▽

◁ *Coprosma acerosa*
The berries of this coprosma may be found brightening the coastal margins, inland river banks and open rocky places. *C. acerosa* is a shrub with slender, tangled branches that can reach 2 m in height. There are about 100 members of the genus *Coprosma*, about half of which are endemic to New Zealand. Most are shrubby plants with an open branching habit, although some are trees, and others are prostrate plants. They are a common feature of our vegetation at all altitudes.

Coriaria sarmentosa ▷
A relative of the well-known tutu (*Coriaria arborea*), this is a shiny-leaved shrub about 1 m high. Growing in open spaces around the coast or in the montane zone, it spreads over large areas, with an underground root system sending up long shoots. This specimen was photographed on rock debris at Palliser Bay, Cook Strait, but the plant occurs in the three main islands.

△
Pomaderris rugosa
Another shrub, growing to 3 m, *P. rugosa* inhabits clay slopes, usually near the sea. It is found in the northern regions, especially around the Coromandel Peninsula.

MATATA, *Rhabdothamnus solandri*
This small shrub is confined to coastal and lowland forests, principally in the North Island. It is endemic to New Zealand, and our only member of the tropical family that also contains the African violet. The orange flower shown here is common, but yellow and red are also seen.

◁ MANGROVE, *Avicennia resinifera*
Growing in thick marine mud, starved of oxygen, the mangrove has a number of special features that help it to survive: breathing roots (pneumatophores) stand erect several centimetres above the mud; leaves can withstand the intense reflection of light off the water; and seeds develop on the tree so that when they drop into the mud the embryos are able to take root quickly, drawing on the food stored in the thick green cotyledons shown above.

△
GLASSWORT, *Sarcocornia quinqueflora*
Glasswort marshes are found in estuaries, tidal flats and lagoons. This plant too can withstand salt water, at times being completely covered. It is less frequently found in rocks and crevices above tidal reach.

CREEPING SELLIERA, *Selliera radicans* ▷
This low-growing plant forms a natural ground cover in coastal muds, sands and rocky places exposed to salt spray from North Cape to Stewart Island.

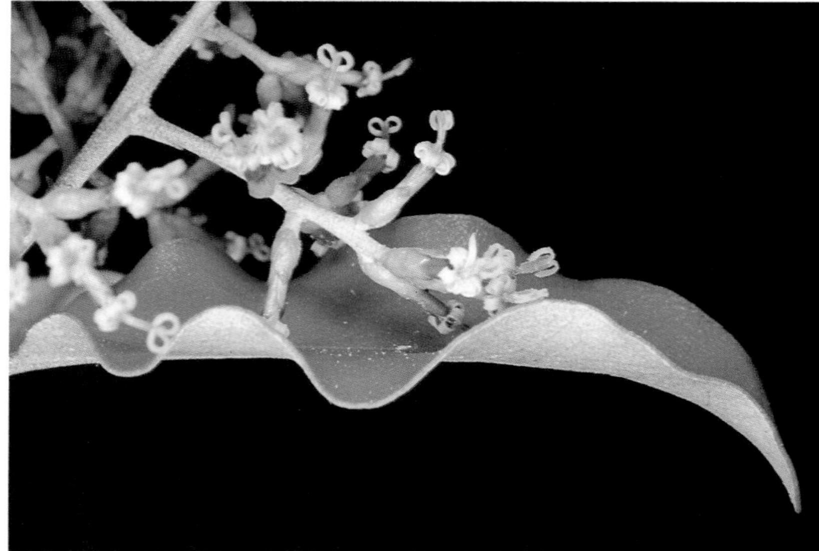

GOLDEN AKEAKE (*Olearia paniculata*) ▷
These tiny, sweet-scented flowers bloom during March and April in coastal shrubland from East Cape south to Greymouth. This hardy shrub is often used for domestic hedges.

Metrosideros carminea
A climbing relative of the pohutukawa, this rata is one of our most brilliant plants. Reaching up as much as 15 m into the tree tops of coastal or lowland forest, it has a natural range from Kaitaia to East Cape and Taranaki, but is now found in only a few places. There are several other species of rata: northern and southern rata (*M. robusta* and *M. umbellata*) can both grow into sizeable trees, but most other ratas are vines. ▽

◁ POHUTUKAWA, *Metrosideros excelsa*
Pohutukawas are renowned for their blaze of crimson or scarlet flowers over the Christmas period. Their spreading crowns and great twining roots dominate cliffs and beaches along the coast north of Poverty Bay and Taranaki. Planted pohutukawas also grow well as far south as Wellington. This tree is one of several ancient pohutukawas on Kawau Island.

NGAIO, *Myoporum laetum* ▷
The straggling branches and light green leaves of the ngaio tree are typical of much of our coastline as far south as Otago. It can grow up to 10 m but more often is a smaller, dome-shaped tree found clinging to exposed cliffs.

Auricularia polytricha
In the warmer, moister coastal forests, dead trees and fallen logs support dense outgrowths of ear fungi. At the time this photograph was taken on Kapiti Island, environmental conditions were suitable for the growth of tens of thousands of these fungi.

Kapiti Island, near Wellington, is an important sanctuary for rare birds like the little spotted kiwi (*Apteryx owenii*). It now appears that the little spotted kiwi may, like the kakapo and takahe, be close to extinction in its last mainland retreat, the forests and shrublands of the Southern Alps and Fiordland. The 500-600 birds on Kapiti Island are now the only known thriving offspring of only five birds transferred to the island in 1913.

CHAPTER FOUR

The Living Forest

◁ THE FOREST CYCLE
Here an old beech tree decays on the forest floor in the upper Grey Valley, north Westland. The collapse of such a tree, possibly hundreds of years old, is just a brief event in the organic cycle of growth, death and decay. The dead tree is a habitat and a source of food, not only for fungi, mosses and small plants that colonise its surfaces, but also a whole host of soil animals that play a vital role in its decomposition and ultimate incorporation into the humus of the forest floor. If this cycle of decomposition and regrowth did not occur, the soil nutrient supply would eventually be exhausted, and the forest would be buried in its own debris.

When the first Polynesian explorers arrived, most of New Zealand was covered in forest, apart from a few small areas of alpine lands, semi-arid grasslands and wetlands. A bewildering variety of species would have confronted the new immigrants. Some of the forest trees would have been familiar, such as pohutukawa, rata and the southernmost of the world's palms, the nikau. Others were probably strange to them – the podocarps and beeches, and hardwoods such as tawa, pukatea and rewarewa.

The New Zealand forest is characterised by a complexity of layers, something like that of a truly tropical forest. A closed canopy of hardwoods such as kamahi, tawa or beech is frequently pierced by the taller trees, such as rimu, rata or kauri, ranging from 30 to 60 m in height. In the subcanopy, lesser trees such as wineberry, mahoe, pate, five-finger, lancewood or the tree ferns, *Cyathea* and *Dicksonia*, compete for light filtering through the canopy. And below this subcanopy, juvenile trees, hard ferns, and a variety of ground plants stand up to a metre above the forest floor where mosses, liverworts, delicate filmy ferns and forest litter cover the soil. Most of the forest trees are evergreen, although a few (kowhai, fuchsia, lacebark or ribbonwood, for example) are deciduous. They characteristically have small leaves, and white, or yellow, often inconspicuous flowers (notable exceptions being pohutukawa, rata, kowhai and kaka-beak).

Traditionally, two major forest groupings have been recognised in New Zealand, one dominated by the conifers (cone-bearing plants) and the other dominated by one or more of the four species of *Nothofagus* or southern hemisphere beech. However, in many areas species from the groups mix in various ways. The conifers are represented in New Zealand by only four families: the araucarians (*Agathis*, the kauri), the cypresses (*Libocedrus*, the mountain and lowland cedars), the podocarps (*Podocarpus*, such as totara or miro; *Dacrycarpus*, the kahikatea; and *Dacrydium*, such as rimu) and the 'celery pines' (*Phyllocladus*). These conifers are relatives of the needle-leaved 'softwoods' of the northern hemisphere, which include pines and firs. The other group are flowering plants, often called 'hardwoods'; besides the beeches there are many other hardwood trees (taraire, tawa, rata, kamahi, hinau and rewarewa, for example) in New Zealand. Some forests consist almost entirely of one group: the mountain beech forests in the South Island, the silver pine/kahikatea swamp forests, or the high-altitude mountain cedar forests above Hihitahi near Taihape. But more common are the mixed forests, containing conifers and hardwoods, for example, or conifers, hardwoods and beeches.

Forest groupings are influenced by a variety of factors – aspect, age, exposure to prevailing wind or frost, geological parent rock, soil conditions, altitude, and temperature variation. New Zealand's vegetation can usefully be described in four altitudinal zones: lowland, montane, subalpine and alpine. But it is an over-simplification to think that lowland and montane forests lie below certain altitudes over the whole 13° of latitude from the subtropical Three Kings Islands to cool-temperate Stewart Island. Rather, several factors, including occurrence of key plants, and broad climatic conditions, also have a bearing on the altitudinal and latitudinal extent of lowland and montane forest throughout New Zealand. In this chapter the forests of the lowland and montane zones are discussed, with subalpine and alpine vegetation covered in Chapters 7 and 8 respectively.

LOWLAND FOREST: North of latitude 38°S, the Kawhia–Opotiki line that marks the southern limit of so many of the subtropical elements in our flora, lowland forest lies below 600 m altitude. In the south-western part of the North Island flanking the Tararua Range (41°S), the upper edge of this forest is 450 m; at Hokitika 300 m; and by latitude 44° 30′S (Martins Bay on the west coast and Timaru on the east coast), most of this lowland forest element has disappeared. (See Fig. 3, p. 152.)

The characteristic form of lowland forest is multi-layered, with podocarps (rimu, matai, or kahikatea) and rata standing high above the canopy of larger hardwoods such as tawa

(*Beilschmiedia tawa*), hinau (*Elaeocarpus dentatus*) and kamahi (*Weinmannia racemosa*). The subcanopy consists of a wide assemblage of small trees – mahoe (*Melicytus ramiflorus*), a five-finger (*Pseudopanax arboreus*), toro (*Myrsine salicina*) or tawheowheo (*Quintinia serrata*), for example. Warmth-loving plants are also a feature of lowland forests: nikau palms and kiekie (*Freycinetia baueriana*), a liane (woody vine) with drooping sword-like leaves, related to the tropical *Pandanus*; or the graceful giant tree ferns, mamaku (*Cyathea medullaris*), whose crowns can clothe whole hillsides.

FOREST EDGE, PUREORA
From the outside, the forest edge can appear an impenetrable wall but, inside, there is order and structure with each tree or plant competing for its place, its own share of food and light.

Epiphytes (or 'perching plants') are considered to be typical of dense tropical forests and yet they abound in our lowland forests, as well as in Chile at the same southern latitudes. Some of the most striking epiphytic plants of the lowlands are the species of *Collospermum* and *Astelia*, members of the lily family. Their immense tufts can be found in the forks of a giant kauri or clinging to a karaka tree on the coastline. Ironically, these epiphytic plants are often found in profusion on an old rata (*Metrosideros robusta*), itself having begun life perched high on another tree. It is possible that this epiphytic habit in our evergreen forests developed as a means of smaller plants getting a 'leg up' to share in the sunshine otherwise filtered out by the leaves of the canopy trees. These epiphytes are absent from the deciduous forests of Europe, presumably because more light filters through to the floor of those forests. Many other epiphytic plants can add to the character of this lowland forest: puka (*Griselinia lucida*) with its grooved roots trailing down the trunks of a carrier tree like puriri (*Vitex lucens*) or cabbage tree (*Cordyline*); or the sweet-smelling epiphytic orchids, *Earina autumnalis* or *Dendrobium cunninghamii*, so often found as a dense tangle of narrow leaves and flowers on the forest floor after a summer storm.

The lowland forest north of latitude 38°S (excluding the higher parts of the Tutamoe, Coromandel and Kaimai Ranges) contains so many trees and plants found only in warmer districts that it is often termed a 'subtropical' forest. Best known amongst them are the giant kauri (*Agathis australis*) and the canopy tree that commonly grows with it, taraire (*Beilschmiedia tarairi*). Many other forest trees, most of them belonging to tropical or subtropical families, are generally restricted to the warmer north; the large and handsome puriri is related to the teak tree of South East Asia and its timber shares some of the strength and durability for which teak is famous; mangeao (*Litsea calicaris*) is only found here; so too is toru (*Toronia toru*), which is, along with rewarewa (*Knightia excelsa*), one of our remaining representatives of the protea family – a family that is so characteristic of other fragments of ancient Gondwanaland such as Australia and South Africa. Several species of the genus *Pittosporum*, makamaka (*Caldcluvia rosifolia*), and tawapou (*Planchonella novo-zelandica*) also add a distinctive note to this 'subtropical' forest. Perhaps one of the most interesting is the small tree, parapara (*Pisonia brunoniana*), New Zealand's sole representative of a family of tropical plants which includes the genus *Bougainvillea*. Parapara ensnares small birds on its sticky ripe fruit. When the birds die, the seeds germinate on the remains, and eventually fall to the forest floor and take root.

But it was the magnificent kauri, reigning supreme above the other trees that gave this lowland forest of the north its particular character. Kauri's fame spread rapidly through the mercantile world of the nineteenth century, and, long before the land was formally acquired by the British Crown, the great kauri forests of the far north were plundered. Today, the only remaining forest associations containing kauri are scattered throughout this northern region – the Coromandel Peninsula, the Hunua and Waitakere Ranges and the Waipoua, Puketi and Omahuta forests in Northland. Once these forests covered almost 1¼ million hectares of the north; now there are probably fewer than 2,000 hectares of dense kauri forest, strictly protected in Waipoua, Warawara, Omahuta and Manaia (Coromandel) forest sanctuaries. In addition, several thousand hectares of mixed forest containing kauri along with rimu, miro, totara, kahikatea, tanekaha, taraire, rewarewa – and even southern rata and kaikawaka – are also protected, especially in Waipoua and Manaia. Under the Government's kauri policy, milling is carefully controlled and the New Zealand Forest Service and the Auckland Regional Authority are making efforts to replant kauri seedlings in old cut-over forests. Perpetuating kauri is not only sound commercial investment for the future. It is also an attempt to conserve one of the world's outstanding trees, perhaps our most notable representative of the ancient forests of Gondwanaland.

Lowland forest throughout the rest of New Zealand has fared little better. The great podocarp/hardwood forests of the Waikato, Taranaki, Rangitikei/Manawatu and southern Hawke's Bay have gone. Pockets of low-altitude beech forests still descend to sea level in a few places – the Eastbourne coastline in Wellington, Abel Tasman National Park, north-west Nelson and Fiordland – but these forests have none of the stature of the tall lowland podocarp/hardwood forests. There are now only two significant tracts of this type of forest left – the rimu forests of the terraces of central Westland and the rimu/totara/kahikatea forests of the volcanic plateau in the central North Island. Both areas have been the subject of bitter forest conservation controversies during the past decade. Both are now the only major podocarp resource remaining for the indigenous timber industry: but to a large number of New Zealanders these places – Okarito and Waikukupa in central Westland and Pureora, Waihaha and Whirinaki on the volcanic plateau – symbolise all that is precious of our Gondwanaland heritage, to be saved at any cost.

MONTANE FOREST: The forests of the montane belt are an upward extension of the lowland forests (Fig. 3). Generally they are less luxuriant, lower in stature and poorer in species. In the western Tararua Range (41°S) the montane zone would lie between 450 m and 900 m, while in northern Fiordland (45°S) the equivalent zone would extend from sea level to around 600 m, thus replacing lowland forest altogether. As the hardwoods of the warmer lowland forest drop out towards its upper limit, kamahi (*Weinmannia racemosa*) and beech (*Nothofagus*) become increasingly dominant. At the lower levels of the montane forest, beech often forms the forest canopy above the other hardwoods, but scattered tall podocarps such as rimu (*Dacrydium cupressinum*) still stand out above it. Towards the upper limit of the montane belt this 'over-storey' of large podocarps ceases and the remaining podocarps, such as Hall's totara (*Podocarpus hallii*), tend to merge with beech in the forest canopy.

At its upper limit the montane forest blends with the lower edges of the subalpine forest, just as the lowland forest gradually merges into the montane belt. The exact point of transition is hard to identify, but the dominance of species of beech is a recognisable feature of montane forest throughout New Zealand. The major exceptions are the slopes of Mt Egmont, the southern Ruahine and northern Tararua Ranges, Stewart Island and the 'beech gap' of 200 km between Lake Brunner and Lake Paringa on the West Coast. Beech forests thrive on catastrophe because of their ability to regenerate vigorously. Thus beech species will quickly revegetate a slope denuded of forest through landslip or windthrow. However, they spread slowly and are only gradually reinvading regions where beech forest was eliminated through major glacial and volcanic events long ago.

To most travellers, our most scenic pure beech forests are those that surround the highways in the upper Buller River region. In these montane valleys – the upper Buller (Kawatiri to Inangahua Junction), Matakitaki (above Murchison), Maruia, upper Inangahua and upper Grey – continuous stands of red beech (in places mixed with silver beech) mantle the landscape. These, and the silver beech forests of the Tuatapere region in western Southland, are the great montane beech forests of New Zealand.

THE REMAINING LOWLAND FORESTS: As supplies of lowland podocarp timber have dwindled, the montane red and silver beech forests have assumed more importance as a substitute that could bridge the gap until the indigenous timber industry has transferred to exotic forest resources. But our lowland forests are considered to be of international as well as local significance because they are probably most like the ancient forests of Gondwanaland. For at least 130 million years, podocarps, beech, araucarians and celery pines have coexisted here in a pattern of continuous evolution unlike that of most other fragments of Gondwanaland. The biota of North Africa and South America have been modified through contact with northern hemisphere organisms, while the forests of Antarctica were swept away by ice. The drier continental climates of Australia and South Africa took them on different evolutionary pathways, through which dryland forests, such as eucalypts and savannahs, developed. The more tropical Gondwanaland remnants – Queensland, New Guinea or New Caledonia – still share this ancient heritage but, in contrast, New Zealand has been more isolated and retained a temperate oceanic climate for a very long period.

FOREST INTERIOR
Tree ferns abound in the shelter of this podocarp/hardwood forest where the common canopy tree is kamahi. Mosses, lichens and epiphytes grow on the trunks, while a rich variety of shrubs and ferns form a layer closer to the forest floor.
▽

LOWLAND FOREST ▷
This lowland forest at Kaitoke in the southern Tararuas shows the typical form when species of podocarp are mixed with hardwoods and beech. Hardwoods such as kamahi, tawa and rewarewa tend to form a canopy along with hard beech. But this canopy is broken in several places through landslips or the collapse of some of the huge old podocarps – rimu, miro and totara – which tower up to 50 m above the forest floor. In a wet, often misty, environment with the annual rainfall over 2,000 mm, this dense forest plays a vital role in regulating water quantity and quality. The catchment serves as Wellington's major water supply.

DENSE PODOCARP FOREST
The largest remaining areas of dense podocarp forest in the North Island are in Pureora State Forest Park and Whirinaki State Forest. The northern part of Pureora, with its deep volcanic soils, carries podocarps so closely packed that they seem to jostle each other as they compete for rooting space and sunlight high above in their crowns. ▷▷

LIMESTONE CAVE, APITI
In areas with a moderate rainfall, such as this in the Rangitikei, soils derived from limestone are very fertile. Here, a rich growth of mosses and ferns drapes the entrance to the cave which the stream has worn in the limestone. Where the light is a little stronger, small orchids and other flowering plants have established themselves in the beds of moss.

FOREST EDGE, ORONGORONGO RIVER
The layers of a lowland podocarp/hardwood forest are shown on this riverbank and terrace community in the Orongorongo River near Wellington. Toetoe lines the riverbank, effectively buffering the vegetation from floodwaters. Behind, tree ferns and manuka and a variety of hardwoods are overtopped by emergent rimu and other podocarps.

KAURI SANCTUARY
Waipoua, in the Tutamoe Range, Northland, is New Zealand's outstanding kauri sanctuary. It was preserved after a bitter public campaign in the late 1940s. The huge spreading crowns of the kauris dominate an under-storey of 'subtropical' luxuriance along the Waipoua River.

◁ BLECHNUM FERNS
Among the plants that greet the traveller as he enters the forest along waterways are blechnum ferns. They are often called 'hard ferns' and grow profusely on stream banks or damp open ground.

NORTH ISLAND KOKAKO,
Callaeas cinerea wilsoni
The kokako, one of New Zealand's most beautiful and ancient birds, is related to the other wattlebirds, the extinct huia and the saddleback. The kokako's numbers have declined drastically, because of predation and the destruction of its forest habitats. It has become a symbol of the campaign for forest preservation, for it is largely confined to some podocarp/hardwood forests of the central North Island and kauri/hardwood forests of Northland.

NEW ZEALAND PIGEON, ▷
Hemiphaga n. novaeseelandiae
The pigeon (kereru) is a conspicuous forest-dwelling bird because of its large size, bright colours and noisy flight. By eating the fleshy seeds of miro, matai and kahikatea, it plays an important role in the distribution and germination of podocarp trees.

TORO, *Myrsine salicina* ▷
This very handsome tree, up to 8m in height, is found in lowland forest. Thus it is most common in the North Island and is not found south of Greymouth. The flowers (about 3mm in diameter) occur in long dense clusters in November.

Pittosporum cornifolium
This *Pittosporum* is rarely seen by the forest visitor. It is an epiphyte which perches on larger trees in the forest canopy. It can be found in lowland forests of the North Island and northern South Island.

LACEBARK, *Hoheria populnea*
Although its natural range is only from North Cape to the Bay of Plenty, lacebark is now popular in gardens throughout the country. In March the tree is festooned in white flowers. The name refers to the 'lace-like' nature of the inner layers of bark.

◁ PYGMY ORCHID, *Bulbophyllum pygmaeum*
This fascinating plant, seen most frequently in the northern parts of the North Island, is the smallest of New Zealand's orchids. As an epiphyte, the pygmy orchid usually forms dense mats high on tree trunks, but in kauri forest it can be found quite low down, and it has even been discovered on exposed coastal rocks.

COCKROACH, *Celatoblatta subcorticaria*
Cockroaches belong to a very ancient order of insects. As scavengers they play an important part in the organic cycle of the forest by eating both animal and vegetable matter.

CROWN FERN, *Blechnum discolor*
This well-known fern can form dense waist-high groves on the forest floor. It is widespread throughout the three main islands as well as the Chatham, Auckland and Campbell Islands, and is a useful marker of the upper limit of montane forest as it is rarely found in subalpine forest.

MOSS ON ROTTING LOG
This moss, probably a species of *Hypnum*, thrives on a decaying log – illustrating one stage in the forest cycle of decomposition and regrowth.

NORTH ISLAND ROBIN, *Petroica australis longipes* △
The North Island robin is one of New Zealand's three subspecies of *Petroica australis* (the other two being the South Island robin and the Stewart Island robin). The extremely rare Chatham Island robin is a different species. The robin is one of the most appealing of the forest birds because of its fearlessness; it will come right up to visitors as it forages for insects, spiders and worms disturbed on the forest floor.

◁ FOREST FLOOR LITTER
As leaves and twigs fall to the forest floor, they are quietly decomposed through an amazing and complex web of life. The forest floor is a sheltered habitat, with high humidity and little temperature variation, and it contains tens of millions of small litter and soil animals per hectare. The most numerous of the soil animals involved in this decomposition chain are the herbivores that consume wood and leaf litter – mites, springtails, hoppers, slaters, millipedes and many insects. Earthworms and nematode worms also help to break down this plant material. Some animals, such as millipedes, ingest huge amounts of litter but extract very little in the way of nutrients. However, their partial digestion is an important link in the decomposition chain, for their excreted pellets then become food for smaller animals or micro-organisms.

FILMY FERNS, *Hymenophyllum*
In the filtered light of the lowland forest interior, delicate filmy ferns have draped themselves over a tree-trunk.

'FAIRY LAMPSHADE' FUNGI, *Mycena*
In the gloomy recesses of the forest floor, clusters of 'fairy lampshade' fungi spring up on the decomposing litter and humus.

HELM'S BUTTERFLY, *Dodonidia helmsii*
This butterfly is relatively little known because it has a very short season. It depends on sunshine for activity, and usually flies high over the tree-tops. It tends to take short, jerky flights, and then rests in the sun for long periods. It frequents beech and mixed beech/kamahi forests north of the Lewis Pass.

FUNGUS,
Hericium coralloides
This fist-sized fungus appears for a few short weeks during the damp winter months. As with other fungi, its structures do not last long, but as they develop they help to decompose the dead trees on which they live. Two weeks after this photograph was taken, the fungus had turned to a brown, slimy jelly.

KAURI BARK
The trunks of more mature kauri trees are kept free of epiphytes by the continual shedding of the attractively patterned bark. This bark can build up as mounds 2 m high at the base of the trunk. Yellow kauri gum can sometimes be seen trickling from between the flakes of bark. This gum was highly valued for the manufacture of paints and varnishes, and it was collected from around the roots or by 'bleeding' the trees.

FUNGUS ON WOOD
The fungi in this genus, *Hypholoma*, grow mostly on dead wood. The caps vary from red to yellow.

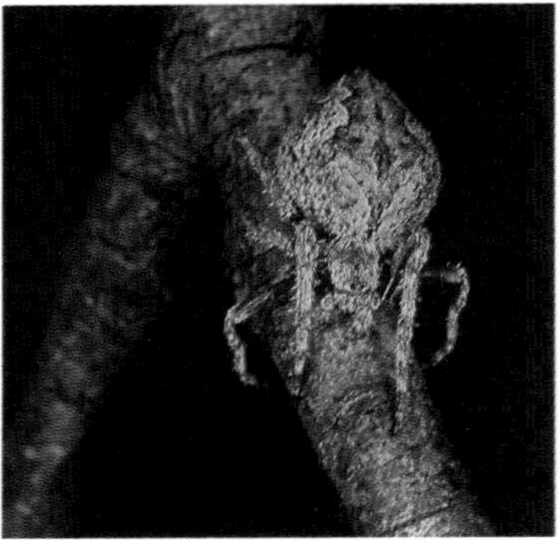

ORBWEB SPIDER, *Araneus pustulosus*
This Australian immigrant inhabits forest margins and open country.

CAVE WETA, *Gymnoplectron edwardsii*
This weta is reasonably common in both North and South Islands, where it is found in caves as well as in forests. Along with other wetas it is considered to be a relic of the fauna of Gondwanaland which has survived in the absence of predators. Before European settlement wetas filled the ecological niche now largely filled by introduced rodents in our forests.
▽

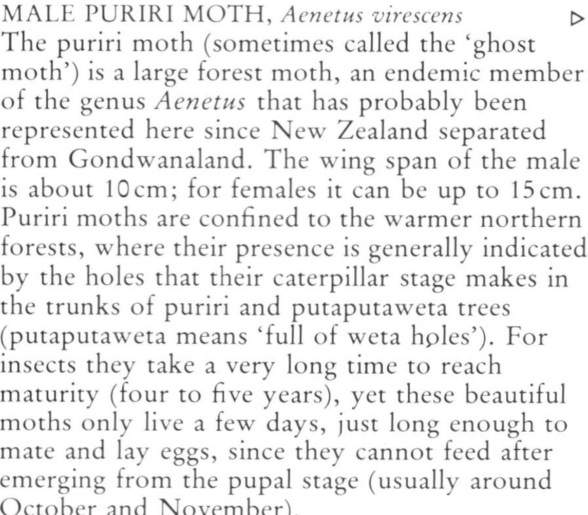

MALE PURIRI MOTH, *Aenetus virescens* ▷
The puriri moth (sometimes called the 'ghost moth') is a large forest moth, an endemic member of the genus *Aenetus* that has probably been represented here since New Zealand separated from Gondwanaland. The wing span of the male is about 10 cm; for females it can be up to 15 cm. Puriri moths are confined to the warmer northern forests, where their presence is generally indicated by the holes that their caterpillar stage makes in the trunks of puriri and putaputaweta trees (putaputaweta means 'full of weta holes'). For insects they take a very long time to reach maturity (four to five years), yet these beautiful moths only live a few days, just long enough to mate and lay eggs, since they cannot feed after emerging from the pupal stage (usually around October and November).

GREAT SPOTTED KIWI, *Apteryx haastii*
◁ The great spotted kiwi, or roa, is one of the three species of kiwi, all of which are nocturnal, forest-dwelling birds. A large bird, weighing up to 3.7kg, it is widely distributed throughout the forests of north-west Nelson and to the west of the Southern Alps. Kiwis have a varied diet: earthworms are the main component, supplemented by many kinds of litter animals as well as berries and leaves.

PALE BROWN LONGHORN BEETLE, *Ochrocydus huttoni*
A native insect, this is sometimes called the 'kanuka longhorn beetle' because kanuka is a favourite host for the larvae. The tunnels excavated by larvae in the living stems of hosts (such as kanuka, manuka, red and mountain beech, and rata) are sometimes subsequently occupied by wetas.

MOREPORK, *Ninox n. novaeseelandiae*
The 'more-pork' cry of this nocturnal forest owl is familiar to most New Zealanders, but few will have ever seen the bird. During the day the morepork roosts in dark hollows in the forest. Its diet consists of insects but it also preys on rodents and small birds.

WHITE PLUME MOTH, *Alucita monospilalis*
The plume moths can be found in forests, their larvae feeding on the leaves of pate (*Schefflera digitata*) and other trees.

WATERCOURSE IN BEECH FOREST
Here, in the montane forests of the upper Grey Valley in north Westland, tall red and silver beech trees tower above a small watercourse.

The distribution of the different species of beech presents anomalies. Red beech (*Nothofagus fusca*) grows on many fertile sites throughout the country, often in association with silver beech (*N. menziesii*); silver beech is rare in the montane forests of the central North Island ranges but is dominant, with hard beech (*N. truncata*), in the Tararua forests. Hard beech characterises the podocarp/beech forests of Nelson and the northern West Coast while black beech (*N. solandri*) is widely distributed on the drier, less fertile sites from East Cape southwards. Mountain beech (*N. solandri* variety *cliffortioides*) is usually thought of as a subalpine forest tree, for it forms the bushline on the drier eastern and central mountains of both islands. However, it is also found at sea level, usually on swampy pakihis or very shallow soils of low fertility. Although it is absent from the Tararua Range, mountain beech probably occupies a wider range of habitats than any other New Zealand tree species because of its tolerance of harsh sites.

Pittosporum ellipticum
The genus *Pittosporum* is widespread in tropical and subtropical parts of the world (except the Americas). There are 26 species of the genus in New Zealand, 18 of them endemic. Most of these species are small trees or shrubs. *Pittosporum ellipticum* is one of the less common, for it is confined to lowland forest in the warmer parts of the North Island, from the Bay of Islands to the Coromandel Peninsula. It is a small tree up to 8 m high with attractive leaves and flowers – features which have given several species of *Pittosporum* a popularity as ornamental plants. The flowers shown here are about 5-10 mm in size.

BELLBIRD, *Anthornis m. melanura*
One of the unforgettable sounds of the lowland forest of New Zealand is the 'bellbird chorus'. In remoter regions on a still morning at the forested edge of a lake, hundreds of bellbirds can still be heard. Their individual chiming songs swell into a wild pulsating melody – the small bells exquisitely tuned that so excited Sir Joseph Banks on a visit to Queen Charlotte Sound. Insects are an important part of their diet, but any nectar-bearing flowers (native and exotic) attract them. Bellbirds inhabit forests and forest margins in all parts of the country south of Auckland.

KIEKIE, *Freycinetia baueriana* ▷ subspecies *banksii*
Kiekie climbs over large trees in the lowland forest. It is a vine related to the tropical *Pandanus* palms whose leaves are used to make thatch and matting.

'GREENHOOD' ORCHID, ▷▷ *Pterostylis banksii*
The genus *Pterostylis* contains some 60 species, of which there are at least 22 in New Zealand. The 'greenhood' orchids are common in damp, shady parts of the forest but can also be found in drier regions under beech or manuka. The flowers contain a tripping mechanism to trap insects; in order to escape they have to crawl over the stigma, and so pollinate it.

LICHEN, *Cladonia floerkeana*
Cladonia lichens are often found on rotting logs in forests, particularly on sunny banks. In the United States, Cladonia lichens are wryly termed 'British soldiers', presumably in reference to the 'redcoats' of the American Revolution.

Coprosma grandifolia △
This shrub or small tree is found in the North Island and northern South Island. The flowers of the many New Zealand coprosmas are inconspicuous and are wind-pollinated, but the fleshy fruits are brightly coloured, and the seeds are distributed by birds.

MISTLETOE, *Peraxilla tetrapetala* ▷
The larger forest mistletoes have all but disappeared from many areas through possum browsing. One, *Trilepidea adamsii*, is now thought to be extinct.

◁◁TOROPARA, *Alseuosmia macrophylla*
Toropara is a shrub found in lowland and montane forests from North Cape to north-west Nelson. These trumpet-like blossoms emit a strong, delicious perfume.

◁TREE FUCHSIA, *Fuchsia excorticata*
The tree fuchsia, kotukutuku, is a major source of food for birds. It is found in lowland and montane forests, where its twisted shape and reddish-brown, papery bark stand out.

BLACK HUNTING WASP, *Salius monarchus*
The black hunting wasp preys upon another group of forest-floor predators – spiders. Typically, the spider is placed in a hole along with one wasp egg. The developing wasp larva then feeds upon the spider carcass.

SILVEREYE, *Zosterops l. lateralis*
The silvereye, like the white-faced heron and welcome swallow, is a relatively recent immigrant to New Zealand, crossing the Tasman Sea from Australia. Silvereyes were first reported in large flocks on the Wellington coast in June 1856 but had probably arrived in the South Island earlier. They are now common throughout the forests of the country, as well as urban gardens and parks.

Gastrodia cunninghamii
This strange orchid has no leaves or chlorophyll and entirely depends for its nutrient supply upon a soil fungus which is a parasite upon the roots of forest trees (usually beech). It is a striking endemic plant 60-80 cm tall, with about 20 flowers on the stalk. It prefers shady areas where the dull, flecked colours of the stalk enable it to merge with the surrounding undergrowth.

TURUTU, *Dianella nigra*
This member of the lily family grows to about 1 m in height and is common along the more open forest margins. The berries ripen in February or March and can be milky white as shown here, but more commonly range from light milky blue to a dark inky blue.

STARRED GECKO
(Heteropholis stellatus)
The starred gecko is an interesting member of an ancient group of reptiles. The New Zealand geckos give birth to live young rather than lay eggs. The only other gecko to do this is in New Caledonia (which separated from New Zealand around 35 million years ago) and the characteristic is probably a longstanding adaptation to cool-temperate climates, since our geckos are the most southern in the world. This member of the gecko family is a canopy-dweller in the beech forests from Nelson to Lewis Pass. There it lives on insect prey, such as flies, moths, cockroaches and caterpillars, particularly where they swarm around flowers. The starred gecko roosts in trees and is rarely seen on the forest floor (as in this photograph), usually during storms or in transit to another tree.

KATYDID, *Caedicia simplex*
The katydid is sometimes called the bush cricket, presumably because of the 'zip . . . zip . . . zip' noise that it makes at night. It belongs to the Orthoptera order of insects, which also contains grasshoppers, locusts and crickets. Katydids inhabit all forms of foliage and may have come from Australia, where they are common.

NORTH ISLAND PIED FANTAIL, *Rhipidura fuliginosa placabilis*
The fantail is one of the most appealing of the forest birds, its fan tail allowing it to perform remarkable flight patterns in pursuit of insects. It is at home in the forest, farmland or suburban garden, for it is a bird that has adapted well to European settlement. The South Island subspecies has a black colour phase as well as the 'normal' pied form.

MONTANE BEECH/HARDWOOD FOREST ▷
Here at sea level in Doubtful Sound, Fiordland, the rain-drenched forests have a montane character and lack the typical warmth-loving species of the true lowland forest of northern regions. Kamahi and silver beech usually form the canopy, although rata and mountain beech are also found at higher altitudes. The subcanopy can be fairly dense, and consists of typical montane species such as broadleaf, the tree fern *Cyathea smithii*, *Pseudopanax* species, *Coprosma foetidissima* and pepperwood (*Pseudowintera colorata*); the common ground fern of montane forests, *Blechnum discolor*, provides most of the ground cover.

MONTANE BEECH FOREST
The character of the montane beech forests is entirely different from that of lowland podocarp/hardwood forest. The interior of the beech forest is less luxuriant, but most noticeable is the lack of any tall podocarps or rata towering above the canopy. Here at an altitude of 400 m in the upper Grey valley the canopy is formed only by beech and is quite regular, clearly showing the angular lines of the glaciated landforms. Red and silver beech, with a small amount of mountain beech on the unfavourable sites, dominate this forest.

◁ BEECH FOREST
Mt Haast (1,587 m) and the Victoria Range form the backdrop to this dense red beech forest in the floor of the Maruia valley (350 m) below Springs Junction. Many of the red beech (*Nothofagus fusca*) trees are over 30 m in height, and the intermingling of this forest with pasture brings a park-like touch to the landscape.

◁ MONTANE BEECH FOREST
This typical beech forest landscape in the upper Buller region of north Westland contrasts with river scenes in lowland forest (see p.57). Here there are none of the tree ferns, the dense under-storey and tall podocarp or kauri trees that distinguish the forests of the lowland zone. Frequent floods in the swiftly flowing Inangahua River have swept clear the granite boulders, but a grove of red and silver beech seedlings has nonetheless established itself precariously on the elemental soil of the streambank. Lacking the complexity and luxuriance of lowland forest, this montane forest may seem monotonous to some travellers. Yet its simple structure has its own beauty, as do the subtle greens of the different species of beech, ever-changing with the seasons.

◁ BEECH FOREST REGENERATION CYCLE
Beech trees are relatively shallow rooting, and are often blown over on these shallow, stony soils. Here an old beech tree has fallen to the forest floor, where it slowly decomposes, its place being taken by a thick growth of beech seedlings. The dead tree is an important part of the life cycle of these forests. It becomes the habitat for a vast range of invertebrates, such as termites, cockroaches, springtails, mites, beetles, wetas and a host of insect larvae. Some of these consume the wood, others consume other animals or their waste products. In turn, forest birds such as kakas tear apart rotting logs to feed on small animals such as huhu grubs. The uprooting of the tree also assists in the regeneration of the forest itself: a greater amount of light can now reach this part of the forest floor; and a quantity of subsoil is often thrown up around the roots of the dead tree, providing ideal conditions for the germination of beech seeds.

BEECH SEEDLING
A tiny seedling of red beech has germinated within a pad of moss on the forest floor. Unless the canopy of the forest is opened sufficiently for the seedling to receive enough light for photosynthesis, it will grow only very slowly, or even stagnate entirely. However, some shade is necessary for the protection of the seedling. The production of seeds is quite irregular, usually at intervals of three to seven years. Heavy seed falls usually occur the year after a hot dry summer. In these years rodent populations can build up quickly with such a plentiful food supply. When the supply is exhausted, the rodents may then ◁ prey upon native wildlife.

△
BEECH SAPLINGS
Gradually the canopy gap is filled by sapling beech trees. The competition between the seedlings for light and soil nutrients is intense and only the stronger seedlings develop to sapling size. These beech saplings are probably about 30-40 years old, and some will not survive to maturity since there is not enough room for the crowns and roots of them all as mature trees.

MATURE BEECH FOREST ▷
The interior of a mature beech forest shows evidence of trees of different ages, the result of the cycles of death and regeneration shown on these pages. The largest red beech trees would be over 100 years, possibly 200. The forest is reasonably open, with no real subcanopy, only isolated beech saplings. The forest floor is covered with beech leaves and a few seedlings; many palatable seedlings will have been eliminated through browsing by deer.

CHAPTER FIVE

Diminishing Wetlands

◁ SWAMP
Pondweed (Potamogeton *species) nestles in the stagnant water between stalks of the sedge,* Scirpus lacustris, *in Rangataua State Forest in the centre of the North Island.*

Swamps, bogs, mires, pakihis, lagoons, marshes, peatlands and upland tarns are all grouped together under the term 'wetlands'. From the perspective of geological time, such areas are only a transitory part of the landscape. The ultimate fate of a wetland is extinction, as it is gradually converted into dry land. Because wetlands always occupy hollows, run-off from the surrounding land deposits sediment in the enclosed waters; this constant water supply, combined with the high nutrient content of the water, makes the wetland a rich environment for vegetation. Plants decay, and the organic debris mixes with the incoming sediment to form an ooze or a peat, and eventually a soil. The process may take thousands of years, but it is a dynamic process with the ecology of the wetland changing as a succession of plants and animals colonises the wetland margin (p.79).

The variety of wetlands found throughout New Zealand is almost infinite. Raupo (*Typha orientalis*) swamps are typical of the sand dune lakes and ponds in farmed areas. The bogs range from huge lowland 'raised bogs' (such as the Kopuatai Peat Dome on the Hauraki Plains, at 100 square kilometres the largest bog remaining in a natural state) to numerous 'blanket bogs' (such as Great Moss Swamp in the cooler, upland basins of the flat-topped mountains of Otago). The 'restiad' bogs, which used to be a feature of the Waikato, are unique to New Zealand. Their name derives from the tall jointed rushes of the Restionaceae family; one of them, *Sporadanthus traversii*, is endemic to northern New Zealand and the Chatham Islands. The one thing that all these wetlands share is the fact that they are ecosystems dominated by a high water-table.

LAKE MAPOURIKA
The margins of this lake in south Westland show the typical zonation of swamp forest vegetation. Sedges give way to flax and ferns, and ultimately tall kahikatea forest.

The significance of wetlands to science and indeed to the economy is little understood by most New Zealanders. They are a major habitat for several kinds of native and introduced fish, amphibia, birds and invertebrates. At least seven species of New Zealand's native freshwater fish inhabit different wetlands; these include the three species of our rare 'mudfishes' (*Neochanna*), a genus of the New Zealand freshwater fish Galaxiidae. Some galaxiids, such as the inanga (*Galaxias maculatus*), are the most common adult of the countless millions of small whitebait which migrate each spring up rivers from the sea, to develop in swamps and creeks. But the mudfish have adapted to live permanently in wetlands, including those that dry up in summer.

Birdlife usually abounds in wetlands, with native and introduced birds often coexisting in the same habitat, but each in slightly different ecological niches. In the open water little black shags dive for fish while black swans graze the totally submerged vegetation; pied stilts, mallard ducks and white-faced herons all inhabit the shallow wetland margins, where they feed on different organisms – soil animals, aquatic plants and insects and fish, frogs and tadpoles respectively. Around the outer margins, pukekos graze both grasses and semi-aquatic vegetation.

Wetlands also help to control flooding, particularly in lowland areas such as the Waikato, Hauraki Plains and the Taieri Plains near Dunedin. The extensive subalpine bogs of upland Otago and Southland are now understood to have an important function in gradually releasing water for the rivers in this region during the summer low-flow period. Peat-forming bogs are a valuable resource for horticulture, particularly our limited areas of *Sphagnum* moss. Peatlands, too, where decomposition is too slow to dispose of the accumulating dead plant material, offer a remarkable record of past vegetation, in the form of plant fossils.

Few who are concerned with the natural environment would be unaware of the losses in wetland area over recent decades. Most accessible peatlands have already been developed or modified, usually for agricultural purposes. From 1954 to 1964 alone, some 160,000 hectares of wetland were reclaimed. By default, it seems, wetlands are still looked upon as potential farmland, and existing legislation does little to protect them. Only two of New Zealand's outstanding wetlands, Farewell Spit and Waituna Lagoon on the Southland coast, have so far been designated 'wetlands of international importance', under an international convention; the great majority have no reserve status at all. New Zealanders have yet to appreciate the diversity that wetlands bring to the landscape, the wildlife that they nourish, their economic importance and their scientific value.

MONTANE BOG
This wetland near the head of the Inangahua River at Rahu Saddle in northern Westland is a fine example of a montane bog. It is covered with a species of the moss, *Polytrichum*, and the occasional summergreen sedge *Carex coriacea*. The reddish-brown spore bodies of the moss can be seen in the middle distance. Shrubs of *Dracophyllum palustre*, manuka, and bog pine (*Dacrydium bidwillii*) have colonised the fringes of the bog.
▽

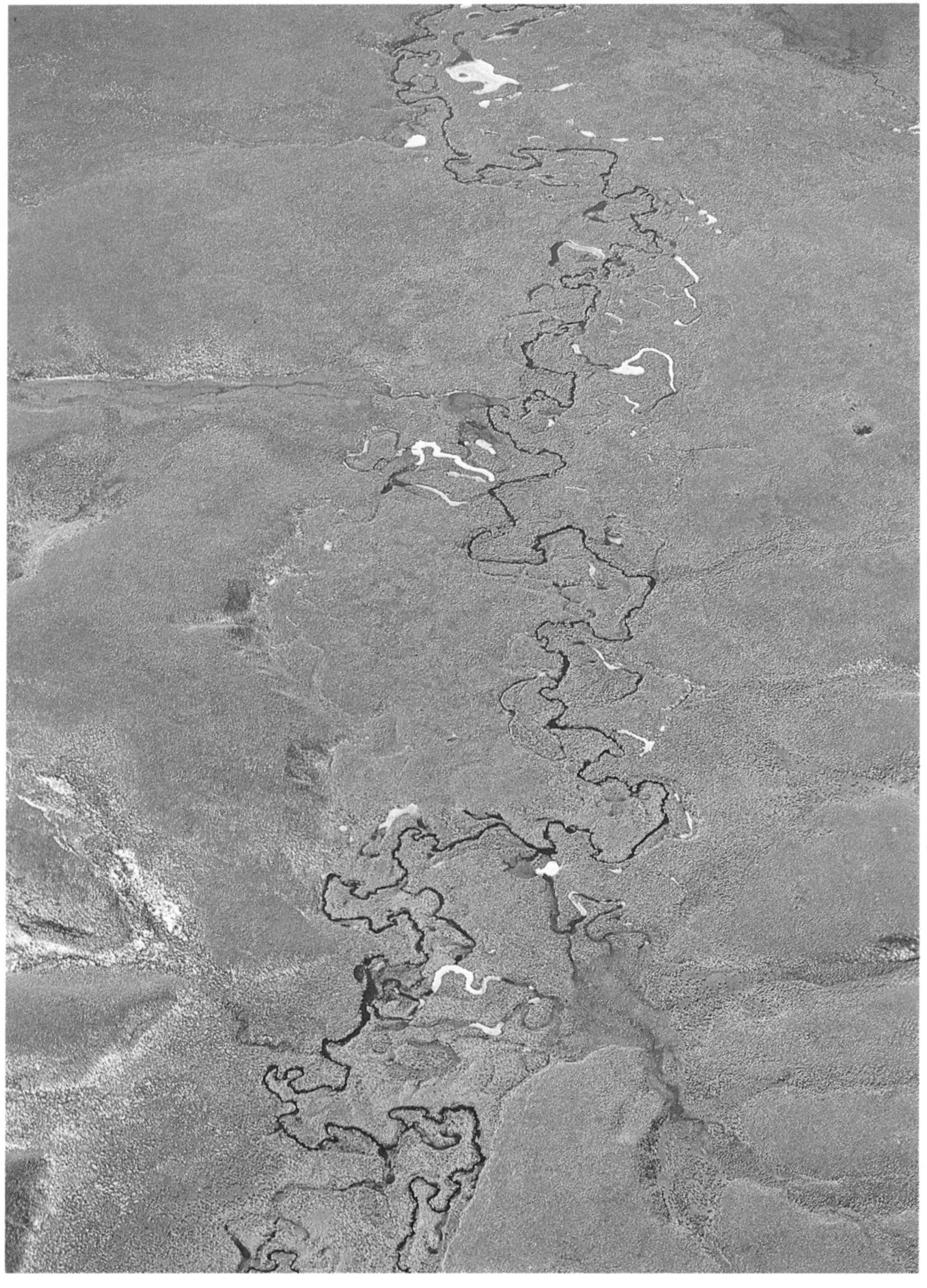

GREAT MOSS SWAMP ▷
The Great Moss Swamp is a large blanket bog (20 square kilometres) lying at 850 m altitude in the remote uplands between the Rock and Pillar and Lammermoor Ranges. The surface vegetation of the swamp itself is dominated by the moss *Sphagnum squarrosum* (which occurs only in the Lammermoor Range) and other *Sphagnum* species. The sinuous shape of the streams indicates the maturity of this smoothed upland surface, which acts as a 'giant sponge' in regulating run-off to the fertile lowlands of the Taieri.

◁PAKIHI, SOUTH WESTLAND
Isolated kahikatea trees (*Dacrycarpus dacrydioides*) and young cabbage trees (*Cordyline australis*) dot a flax swamp in south Westland. In the distance on the fringe of the swamp, a dense forest of kahikatea and other podocarp trees, such as rimu, can be seen. This swamp is a more fertile variant of the large West Coast wetlands commonly called pakihis, and it shows one form of plant succession around a wetland.

Typically, a pakihi is covered with wire rush (*Empodisma minus*) growing on small mounds with mosses in the wet hollows; at the fringe of the pakihi large tussocks of *Gahnia rigida* can be found among an open canopy of young manuka. The next zone is a dense manuka woodland interspersed with young trees such as silver pine, rimu, or kamahi. The manuka then grades into a typical silver pine (*Dacrydium colensoi*) forest about 12 m tall, although characteristic wetland species such as shrubs of *Phyllocladus aspleniifolius* variety *alpinus* and a ground cover of hard fern (*Blechnum*) and tangle fern (*Gleichenia*) are still common. Stands of young rimus take over from the silver pine, while the last, and oldest, zone in the succession is the surrounding mature lowland forest of rimu, kahikatea and miro.

CUSHION BOG ▷
Small bogs can be found even at high altitudes where they often support more prolific plant life because moisture is rarely limiting. This small flush at 1,400 m on the slopes of the Old Man Range in Central Otago contrasts with the depleted vegetation on the surrounding slopes. A green mat of *Drapetes lyallii* covers the wet hollow. On the sheltered banks some of the characteristic plants of the region can be seen – tussocks of *Chionochloa macra*, cushions of *Raoulia hectori* and the flowers of *Celmisia viscosa*.

DRAGON-FLY, *Diplacodes bipunctata*
This colourful dragon-fly was photographed on the shallow waters of the Kai Iwi Lakes in Northland. Elsewhere on the West Coast of New Zealand, they have been observed in swarms, perhaps indicating that they regularly cross the Tasman Sea from Australia.

SWAMP MUSK, *Mazus radicans*
Swamps and bogs often contain small attractive plants such as this swamp musk, a perennial herb found from Rotorua southwards.

LITTLE SHAG, *Phalacrocorax melanoleucos brevirostris*
A sudden wind has wakened this little shag, causing it to erect its crest. The white throat of this rather timid bird has given rise to its other name, 'white-throated shag'. Little shags prefer freshwater rivers, lakes and swamps, but are also common around the coast.

◁ MIRROR LAKES
Wetlands can be found in all the other natural environments – on coasts or tussock grasslands, in forests or alpine regions. These small lakes, fringed with flax, tussock and matagouri, contrast with the surrounding beech forest so typical of Fiordland.

AUSTRALASIAN BITTERN, *Botaurus stellaris poiciloptilus*
The bittern is at home in swamps and wetlands throughout Australia, New Zealand and New Caledonia. As swamps have been converted to farmland, their habitat has been reduced dramatically. If disturbed, their colouring and motionless stance with bill pointed skyward make them very difficult to detect. Only when they are cornered do they adopt the threatening posture shown here.

△
PUKEKO, *Porphyrio p. melanotus*
Unlike the bittern, the pukeko has adapted well to landscape changes and is now a common inhabitant of farmlands, provided there is enough cover for breeding. It is distributed widely throughout Australia, Tasmania and New Zealand. The pukeko runs swiftly, swims well, and can fly when it has to. It particularly likes raupo swamps, where it builds nests up to 80cm high from dead raupo leaves. Soft shoots, berries, insects, young birds and frogs make up its diet.

POND, KARIOI FOREST
Ponds like this one are not uncommon in the altered landscape of pine plantations. *Pinus radiata* forest extends to where the water-table level restricts growth. In earlier years, native swamp forest, predominantly kahikatea, would have crowded the swamp edge. Flax, carex and raupo would have colonised the wetter parts of such a swamp ecosystem. Now, introduced willows frame the foreground, while the red water fern (*Azolla rubra*) and duck-weed (*Lemna minor*) float on the surface.

BLACK SWAN, *Cygnus atratus*
Black swans were first introduced from Australia in 1864, and are now firmly established in swamps and lagoons throughout New Zealand, including the Chatham Islands. They prefer larger lakes where they can feed close to the shore and extract water weed by dipping with their long necks.

WHANGAMARINO SWAMP ▷
Willows of the genus *Salix* have become a familiar sight alongside rivers, lakes and swamps in New Zealand since they were introduced in the late 1800s. Where native vegetation has been destroyed, they grow quickly, even invading flax and carex swamps. Willows now abound in the Whangamarino Swamp and the nearby Waikato River. While ducks, pukekos and shags can all thrive in this modified environment, the native fernbirds, still found in the swamp, prefer more open habitats, such as beds of rush and fern.

PIED STILT, *Himantopus h. leucocephalus* △△
These spindly waders are a common sight in wetlands and coastal areas around the country, picking their way delicately around the edge of a lagoon, swamp or coastal sandbank. With their long bills they probe shallow waters for insects, shellfish, worms and other small animals. After summer breeding, they usually migrate from inland areas, often to the northern harbours and inlets. The development of farmland appears to have encouraged breeding, and the population has increased since European settlement.

LITTLE BLACK SHAGS,
Phalacrocorax sulcirostris
With a more restricted breeding range than the little shag, this species is nonetheless widespread in lakes and estuaries north of Lake Taupo. It is rare in the south. These birds nest in colonies and can be seen fishing in groups, apparently combining forces to increase the catch.

CHAPTER SIX

Tussock Country

The words 'tussock country' conjure up for most of us the great open spaces of the South Island high country – Molesworth, the Mackenzie Country and Maniototo Basin in Central Otago. Here the forests seem to have retreated to the distant mountains to the west or remain behind as scattered remnants in the eastern coastal regions. The tussock grasslands are New Zealand's modest equivalent of the other great temperate grasslands – the prairies of North America and the pampas of Patagonia.

The tussock grasslands are an indigenous habitat in which man has learned, eventually, to pasture his stock without completely destroying the dominant plants. Early exploitation, such as the indiscriminate burning and over-stocking of the Rakaia grasslands, so aptly and enthusiastically described in the writings of Lady Barker, led to depleted grasslands scarred by various forms of soil erosion. Yet, ironically, it was fire in prehistoric and pre-European times that allowed tussock grasses to colonise land that was formerly forested in drier regions of both islands, but particularly the hilly lands and basins on the eastern side of the Southern Alps. Without periodic fires most of these grasslands would have been gradually invaded by shrubs, to be ultimately transformed back into forest. Tussock grasslands evolved and flourished with fire, and were able to withstand the effects of native browsing animals – grasshoppers and birds such as moa, takahe and occasionally kakapo that 'chewed' the leaves of tussock grasses. But it was the deadly combination of fire and heavy stocking of European sheep and cattle (and, later, the invasion of rabbits) that subsequently led to the deterioration of most of the vast area of South Island tussock grassland (nearly 5 million hectares), especially in the montane and subalpine zones.

Today, most of this land is grazed within high country pastoral runs, although some of the steeper and more eroded land is retired for soil and water conservation. These grasslands are still a predominantly indigenous habitat, even though they are extensively grazed, top-dressed with fertiliser, and oversown with introduced grasses and clovers. Their tawny landscape has been celebrated by poets and captured by artists. This is the country explored by the noted Otago surveyor, John Turnbull Thomson; the grasslands and mountain hinterlands that inspired Samuel Butler's *Erewhon*; and the harsh, exposed land which yielded the fickle precious metal, gold, to thousands of miners in the great Otago gold-rushes of the 1860s. Although much of the vegetation has changed, the bold landforms and the open character of the land still remain much as they were 150 years ago.

The name 'tussock' probably comes from the Old English word *tusk*, meaning 'a tuft of hair'. It is now used to describe southern hemisphere grasses of a characteristic 'tufted', or bunched, habit. The tussocks found in the drier, low-altitude grasslands are small, usually 30-60 cm in height, and are best referred to as 'short tussocks'; they belong to genera such as *Festuca* and *Poa* which are common in other temperate grasslands, or to the predominantly Australian genus, *Rytidosperma*. The larger tussocks can be up to 2 m in height as well as diameter, their long narrow blades often arching across smaller herbs and grasses in their shelter. These are the 'tall tussocks' of the genus, *Chionochloa*, which is virtually endemic to New Zealand. Only one other species has been described (from the summit of Mt Kosciusko, the highest mountain in Australia), although other species of *Chionochloa* may be found eventually in the mountains of other Gondwanaland fragments such as New Caledonia or New Guinea.

TALL TUSSOCK GRASSLANDS: The tall tussocks of the alpine herbfields and grasslands are generally called 'snow tussocks' to distinguish them from lower-altitude tall tussocks, such as the 'bush tussocks' (*C. conspicua* and *C. cheesemanii*) and red tussock (*C. rubra*). The snow tussocks that are essentially confined to the wettest areas of the axial ranges are more appropriate to the alpine zone and are discussed in Chapter 8.

To the east of the Southern Alps, the higher-altitude tussock grasslands are dominated by two

◁ NORTH ROUGH RIDGE
*From North Rough Ridge between the Ida Burn and the Wether Burn, the land slopes gently down to the Maniototo Basin. Beyond lies the long, flat summit of the Rock and Pillar Range. This is the heartland of Central Otago, with an uninterrupted view of open basins and tussock-covered mountain ranges in every direction – Raggedy, St Bathans, Hawkdun and Ida Ranges as well as the Kakanui and Dunstan Mountains. The vegetation is dominated by short tussocks (*Festuca novaezelandiae*) with clusters of the prickly golden spaniard (*Aciphylla aurea*) among the outcrops of schist on the summit of the ridge.*

HIGH COUNTRY SHEEP MUSTER
Much of the pastoral land in the South Island high country is montane tussock grassland.

species: slim snow tussock (*C. macra*) is abundant from low to high altitudes north of the Rakaia to the head of the Wairau River; south of the Rakaia it is usually found only at higher altitudes, particularly on shady or southerly slopes. The other species, narrow-leaved snow tussock (*C. rigida*), has a much wider altitudinal and temperature range than any of the other species. It can be found at sea level in south-east Otago, is present on Banks Peninsula, and ranges over the terraces, downs and mountain slopes of the lowland, montane and subalpine zones of South Canterbury, Otago and parts of Southland.

There are many more herbs than grasses growing in these tall tussock grasslands, but they generally provide only a small percentage of the ground cover. Shrubs such as the mingimingis, *Leucopogon suaveolens* and *L. fraseri*, are sometimes common as well as scattered *Pimelea*, the spiny wild irishman or matagouri (*Discaria toumatou*) and native brooms (*Carmichaelia*). The tall, golden-coloured spaniard ('speargrass') *Aciphylla aurea* stands out, its tall inflorescence warning the visitor of the sharp leaves which merge so well with the blades of tussock. Careful exploration among the tussocks will reveal many delicate herbs – native violets, harebells and geraniums – each occupying a niche within this sheltered environment between the tussocks.

SWEET BRIAR
The dry climate of Central Otago tussock grasslands suits the introduced shrub sweet briar, Rosa rubiginosa, *the traditional source of rose hip syrup.*

The other major species of tall tussock is red tussock (*C. rubra*), which is a feature of tussock grasslands from the central North Island southwards. It covers many of the youthful landforms of the volcanic plateau of the North Island; it grows at lower elevations than the other tall tussocks in both Canterbury and Otago, often in damper valley floors or slopes with poor drainage; and the red tussocklands of the Southland plains and hills were once a joy to behold. Now they have mostly been developed into pasture, and the traveller from Mossburn to Te Anau and Fiordland National Park today can gain only a fleeting impression of what must have been one of the most striking scenes in primitive New Zealand. On windy, sunny days, large shaggy tussocks almost glint with a bronze lustre as they sway across the broad Gorge Hill watershed between the Takitimu and Eyre Mountains.

Although the red tussock grasslands of the North Island are small in comparison to the South Island high country, they are amongst our most dramatic landscapes. These are the grasslands that the traveller passes through along the Desert Road. Unlike the red tussock country of the South Island, most of this volcanic landscape is protected as part of Tongariro National Park. (See Chapter 9.) However, another impressive piece of tussock country, the top of the inland Patea road between Taihape and Napier, has disappeared under the plough within the last 15 years. But three distinct areas of considerable botanical diversity still remain in this remote land of high plateaux, gorges and intermontane basins dominated by red tussock. The Ngamatea Plateau in the upper Taruarau River, the upper Moawhango valley including the Mt Azim Gorge, and the Reporoa Bog region of the north-west Ruahine Range each contains 350-400 different indigenous plant species. The three grassland areas have a combined indigenous flora of some 700 species, of which 50 occur nowhere else in the North Island. Such richness certainly gives the lie to any claim that tussock grasslands are 'biological deserts'. Much of the area has probably never been completely forested during post-glacial times and, consequently, these grassland communities have served as refuges for many small plants. However, the introduced lodgepole pine poses a serious threat as it continues to invade the western regions of these tussock grasslands.

TUSSOCK LANDSCAPES: CENTRAL OTAGO AND CANTERBURY: The mountains of inland Marlborough and Canterbury, with their moraines, glacial and river terraces, screes, fans and steep, incised valleys, are well known to visitors to Nelson Lakes, Arthur's Pass and Mt Cook National Parks. Their rocks consist in the main of alternating layers of very hard sandstones and siltstones, called greywacke and argillite (Chapter 1), which have been uplifted, folded and fractured so that they tend to shatter to angular fragments in the climatic extremes of these rugged mountains.

But the landscape begins to change subtly as one travels south out of the *Festuca* grasslands of the Mackenzie Basin, climbing up the Ahuriri valley to the striking tussock grassland of Lindis Pass. Here the traveller can pass through magnificent rolling country covered by *Festuca matthewsii* and the snow tussock, *Chionochloa rigida*. In this region, the St Bathans and Hawkdun Ranges form a mountain barrier between Canterbury and Otago, a watershed between the vast

Waitaki and Clutha River catchments. But Lindis Pass marks more than just a provincial boundary; it is also a geological boundary, for here the greywacke of Canterbury abruptly gives way to the schist of Otago. Schist is a more heterogeneous rock than greywacke, with some layers more resistant to weathering than others. It is these flat, attractive slabs of schist rock that give so much character to the landscape of Central Otago, from the shining metallic grey of the stream beds to the many stone huts, relics of gold-rush settlements – the Bendigos and Blackstone Hills of 120 years ago.

It is landscape of great variety. In the eastern regions the ranges – Lammerlaw and Lammermoor, Umbrella, and Rock and Pillar – have been smoothed out and are generally described as 'uplands'. Here, moist south-easterly winds occasionally bring rain and snow, and *Chionochloa rigida* predominates; but, further inland, the basins of the upper Taieri, Clutha and Manuherekia are very dry, with annual precipitation as low as 350 mm. In other areas the schist bedrock has been tilted on an angle and weathering has given the 'fretted landscape' of rock outcrops and shallow drainage streams so characteristic of the western slopes of the Dunstan Mountains and the aptly named Raggedy Range, Knobby Range, and Rough Ridge. Where the schist bedrock is more horizontal, weathering has produced columns of rock called 'tors'. On the smooth summits of some of the highest block mountains, such as the Pisa and Old Man Ranges and the Dunstan Mountains, spectacular tors like Leaning Rock and the Obelisk rise as high as 15 m. Everywhere the tussocks complement rather than obscure these dramatic landforms by the simplicity of their growth habit.

From a distance these short tussock and tall tussock grasslands in the rain-shadow of the Southern Alps look uniform and botanically uninteresting but closer contact reveals a host of interesting plants. Wildlife can be found – skinks and geckos, birds such as pipits and skylarks with their lovely song carrying across a quiet landscape. Rare birds such as the black stilt can be seen in some of the rivers and deltas, and the harrier hawk soars across a landscape which holds little to impede his view of prey.

THE ORIGIN OF THE TUSSOCK GRASSLANDS: Much of this mid-altitude tussock grassland (up to 1,000 m) was formerly forested: in the montane regions by Hall's totara (*Podocarpus hallii*) with some *Nothofagus*; at lower altitudes, as on the Canterbury Plains, probably by podocarps such as matai in a mosaic with kanuka. About 700-800 years ago, fires (probably of Maori origin) began to destroy this forest. In the drier regions, a short tussock grassland of *Poa colensoi* and *Festuca novae-zelandiae* would have developed as a result of these light-demanding species migrating out from streambeds and enclaves within the forest. At the other extreme of altitude and moisture, the alpine snow tussocks, *C. rigida* and *C. macra*, probably slowly moved down to ultimately cover the subalpine, montane and the moister lowland zones. Red tussock would have colonised the damper regions such as valley bottoms and low-lying basins and climatically suitable regions like the cool moist Southland plains.

The transformation of most of this lower-altitude grassland from tall tussocks to the more palatable short tussocks has occurred since European settlement. Much of the severe erosion in the high country has occurred in this midslope zone of 'vegetation weakness' around 1,000 m – a zone where short tussocks reach their tolerance limits and tall tussocks have difficulty colonising because most of the more fertile topsoil has been stripped away by the combined effect of wind, rain and frost. It is here, not in the high alpine zone, that conservation measures are most necessary to restore the tussock grasslands to their former vigour. The area of unmodified montane tussock grassland in reserves is minute, the lowland tussockland remnants almost negligible. Despite well-intentioned conservation policies, the economic imperative seems to carry the day. These magnificent indigenous tussock landscapes are disappearing inexorably, the plants banished to their former mountain and streambed domains. But it is not the former forests that are replacing them, but introduced pastures. In the long term the tussock, so well adapted ecologically for a harsh environment, has many important roles to play – as a source of forage, a shelter plant for more nutritious introduced grasses, a protective cover against soil erosion, and a visual reminder to us of a special group of indigenous plants that have made their own distinct contribution to the character of our land.

IDA RANGE FOOTHILLS
Here, in the foothills of the Ida Range, the topography is subdued. Long ago the greywacke of the Ida and Hawkdun Ranges was eroded, and deposited as sands and clays in the depressions between the ranges. Subsequent faulting in the late Tertiary caused the ranges to be uplifted and tilted, leading to further erosion; more gravel and sand poured into the valleys, covering the earlier sediments. During the Pleistocene, glaciers again swept more debris into the basins. All this material has since been moulded into a rolling landscape by wind, rain, snow and frost. The smoothness of these hills, covered in fescue tussock and scattered narrow-leaved snow tussock (*Chionochloa rigida*), contrasts with the fretted, craggy surfaces of the schist mountains, such as Raggedy Range, nearby.

Previous page
THE MANIOTOTO
From the slopes of Mt Buster in the Ida Range, the whole sweep of the Maniototo Basin is visible, from the Kakanui Mountains to the distant Rock and Pillar Range.

COMMON GRASS ORCHID, *Prasophyllum colensoi*
Small orchids find shelter among the tussocks of the uplands. These plants are 20-25 cm high and their solitary leaves look like onion leaves. There are usually about 20 small flowers on each stem.

IDA RANGE
In the vicinity of Dansey Pass on the Kakanui Mountains, the outcrops of tilted rock contrast with the smooth outline of the Ida Range in the distance. Nearby, a lonely road winds across the Kakanui Mountains, the old miners' route from the Waitaki to the gold-diggings of the Maniototo.

GRASSHOPPER, *Phaulicridion marginale*
New Zealand's grasshoppers are mostly endemic and generally confined to the subalpine and alpine grasslands. They are perhaps the most energy-efficient herbivores in the tussock grasslands, for they spend 90 per cent of their active hours basking in the sunshine and only expend the minimum energy in feeding and moving. In these adaptations they are true conservationists, ensuring their own survival and minimising their impact on their grassland habitat.

BROOM, *Carmichaelia petriei*
This native broom is confined to the montane regions of the South Island, where it grows in open places particularly in tussock grasslands. Like the other 16 or so species of *Carmichaelia*, it is a member of the legume family and is able to fix atmospheric nitrogen in the soil through bacteria associated with its roots. This capacity gives brooms a competitive advantage in colonising mineral soils low in humus – such as eroded soils in the tussock grasslands.
▽

SUBALPINE MIST ▷
In the long term the most valuable product of these tussock grasslands and uplands is neither gold nor wool – but water. Water was necessary for sluicing for gold and it is essential today for irrigation of orchards and pastures in semi-arid Central Otago, and for the generation of hydroelectricity on the Clutha River. Scientific studies have shown that a natural undisturbed cover of vegetation is crucial if these tussock grasslands are to yield the maximum amount of water. Snow tussocks are particularly useful because of their ability to accumulate moisture by 'intercepting' mist with their long grooved blades.

COMMON BROWN SKINK, *Leiolopisma nigriplantare maccanni* ▷
On the dry summits of the lower ranges of Central Otago, flat slabs of schist and groves of golden spaniard offer plenty of cover for the common brown skink. Here, too, insect food is plentiful.

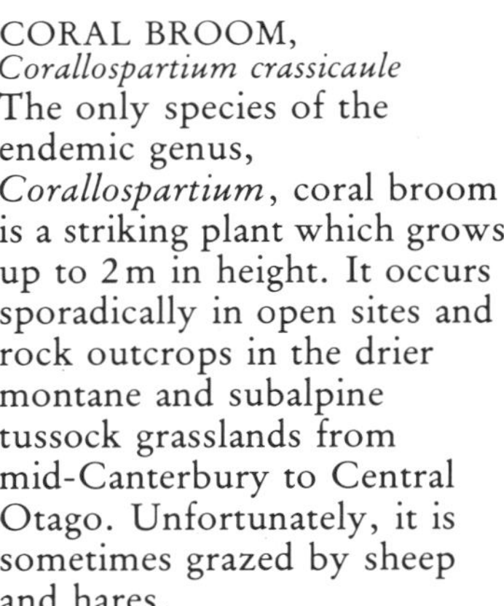

CORAL BROOM, *Corallospartium crassicaule*
The only species of the endemic genus, *Corallospartium*, coral broom is a striking plant which grows up to 2 m in height. It occurs sporadically in open sites and rock outcrops in the drier montane and subalpine tussock grasslands from mid-Canterbury to Central Otago. Unfortunately, it is sometimes grazed by sheep and hares.

RAGGEDY RANGE
The summit of the Raggedy Range illustrates well the type of fretted landscape that is exposed when erosion strips away the deposits of gravel or layers of weathered schist. The drainage patterns are very subtle in this semi-arid environment. Some small herbs and grasses contribute to the greenness evident in the depressions, but mostly the vegetation is a sparse cover of heavily grazed *Festuca* and *Poa* and low cushions of 'scabweed' (*Raoulia australis*).

BRANCHES AND LICHEN
Dead, woody plants decompose only slowly in this semi-arid climate and the profuse coverage of the slowly growing red lichen, *Haematomma puniceum*, would indicate that this *Hymenanthera alpina* has been dead for some time.

Raoulia hookeri
Soft, silvery mats of *Raoulia hookeri* can be found in open sites in tussock grasslands. Here the cushion plant even manages to spread itself across a bare schist rock surface, its leaves thickened and covered in fine, woolly hair for protection against moisture loss and extremely cold temperatures.

CLUTHA VALLEY AND KNOBBY RANGE
The Clutha River has progressively cut down into this landscape, planed smooth long ago by the action of ice, water and wind. In this view from the eastern flanks of the Old Man Range the glacial terraces above the gorge of Lake Roxburgh can be seen. These surfaces are mantled with windblown silt (loess) derived from the exposed surfaces as ice retreated during the waning stages of the Pleistocene glaciations. Above the terraces lie the dissected slopes of the Knobby Range, a complex mixture of schist outcrops and loess-derived soils.

Hymenanthera alpina
Hymenanthera alpina is one of the hardiest shrubs growing in the dry, eastern tussock grasslands. It is usually no more than 60 cm high and its stiff, woody branches (with spines on the ends) form an interlacing network. Its characteristic habitat is exposed rocky places, over quite a wide altitudinal range (200-1,800 m). The small, thick leaves are an adaptation to resist moisture loss and it is quite common to see lichens, such as this *Teloschistes velifer*, colonising the stiff branches.

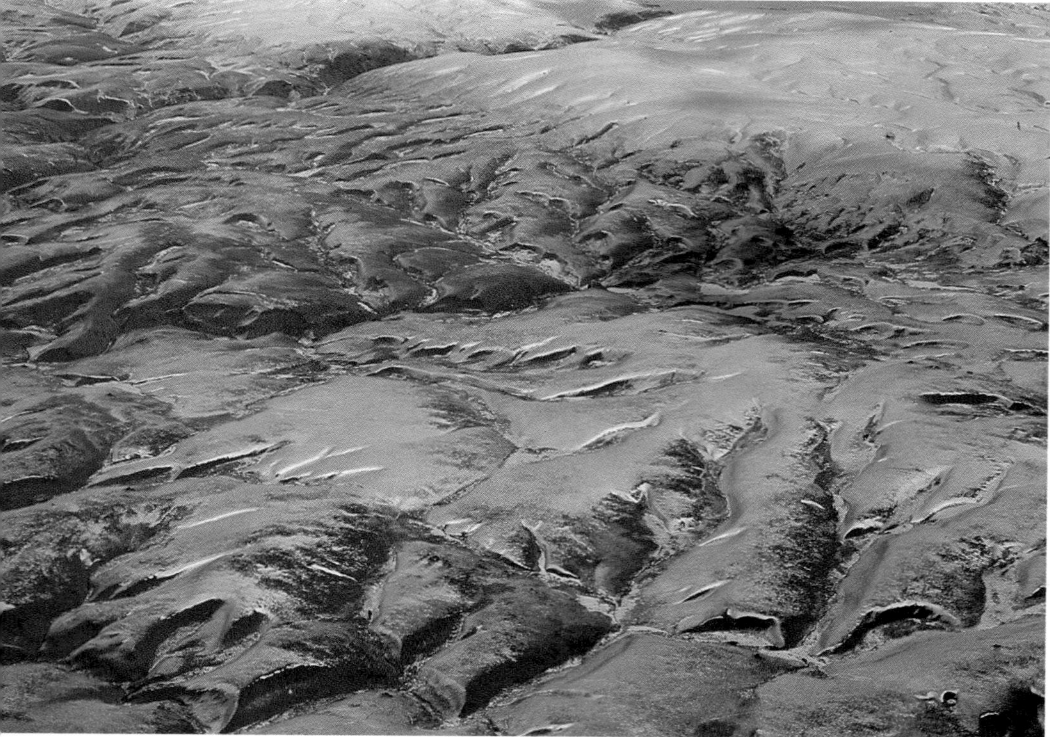

△
ROCK AND PILLAR RANGE IN WINTER
The gentle upland landscape of the schist Rock and Pillar Range contrasts with the steeper greywacke slopes of the Hawkdun Range in the distance beyond the Maniototo Basin. Although the summit of the Rock and Pillar Range is only around 1,300 m in altitude, these broad plateaux retain large quantities of snow. As these tussock uplands surround semi-arid intermontane basins, this winter snow is also the potential irrigation water of spring and summer. The summits of the Rock and Pillar Range were smoothed, probably by deep erosion, as long ago as the Cretaceous period.

LAMMERLAW RANGE IN WINTER
The Lammerlaw Range in the eastern Otago uplands is another smooth tussock-covered upland area where loess has accumulated on weathered schist; tors and rocky outcrops are not apparent. The light blanket of snow highlights the fault traces running across the landscape and the high incidence of back-cutting by short streams to form small steep cirques where shelter, shade and moisture conditions create an entirely different environment for plants.

UPPER TAIERI GORGE
The drainage patterns in these uplands of Otago are generally quite shallow on the broad ridges. However, in the east, the uplands are sometimes dissected by deep, steep-sided valleys like the upper gorge of the Taieri shown here. Yet such gorges are relatively few in number and are separated by easy, rolling ridges mantled in loess and often covered with the narrow-leaved snow tussock, *Chionochloa rigida*. The climate on these uplands is moister than that of the ranges of Central Otago. Occasional moist south-easterlies bring foggy conditions to the surrounding Lammerlaw and Lammermoor Ranges.

Bulbinella gibbsii variety *balanifera*
The colourful flowers of *Bulbinella* (commonly called 'Maori onion') stand out on the tussock grasslands. These members of the lily family are widespread in montane to low alpine regions, where large numbers often grow in peaty grasslands and bogs.

◁ LINDIS PASS
Lindis Pass, the boundary between the Mackenzie Basin and the upper Clutha basins, is one of the least modified tussock grassland landscapes that can still be seen from a major highway. Here the shorter *Festuca matthewsii* grows alongside the taller *Chionochloa rigida* snow tussocks. Regrettably, only part of this landscape is protected, in one of our few tussock grassland reserves.

◁ KAKANUI FOOTHILLS
The foothills of the Kakanui Mountains, dimpled in the low-angle sunlight, express so well the simple beauty of Central Otago. Fescue tussock covers this stable, rolling landscape which shows no evidence of recent erosion. Water races, relics of the goldmining era, gently slope their way down the flat-topped ridges in the foreground to some long-abandoned destination.

◁ MATAGOURI, *Discaria toumatou*
Matagouri was given the name 'wild irishman' by the early runholders of the tussock country, presumably because of the tough, prickly nature of the shrub. It is one of the most characteristic plants of the drier regions in the tussock grasslands, especially riverbeds and alluvial terraces, where it sometimes forms a spiky, impenetrable shrubland with bushes up to 5 m tall.

△
SUMMITS OF HAWKDUN RANGE
The Hawkdun Range lies at the remotest northern corner of Central Otago. Unlike the usual schist ranges of the Otago tussock grasslands, the Hawkdun Range consists mainly of greywacke, like the tussock-covered high country of Canterbury. The flat summits of this part of the range show the old peneplain surface which has since been dissected by waterways to give the characteristic steep-sided streams.

◁ HEADWATERS OF THE OTEMATATA RIVER
The upper reaches of the Otematata River (a tributory of the Waitaki River) lie in a strongly faulted zone of greywacke and semi-schist wedged among the Hawkdun, Ida and St Marys Ranges. This sinuous gorge winding among steep eroding slopes can be contrasted with the other tussock gorge of the Taieri in the schist uplands of eastern Otago (p. 95).

CHAPTER SEVEN

Towards the Bushline

The subalpine forests dominate our indigenous landscape simply because they are so obvious. The forested backdrop to much of our farmland lies in the subalpine zone, whether it be the upper forest belt on Mt Egmont as seen from anywhere in Taranaki; Hauhungaroa Range from the King Country or West Taupo; the Ruahine Range from the Rangitikei or Hawke's Bay; or the Tararua Range from the Horowhenua or Wairarapa. The South Island, in particular, is a rugged landscape, with steepland (land with slopes greater than 28°) forming 57 per cent of the island. Much of this steepland lies along the Southern Alps, where the harder, older greywacke and schist rock has been carved into steep streams and sharp ridge crests. But it is also found in other, very different regions: the young, recently uplifted (geologically speaking) Kaikoura Ranges; or the relatively stable mountains – Fiordland, the Tasman Mountains of north-west Nelson, and the Paparoa Range of northern Westland – where the rocks, such as granites and gneisses, are predominantly old, hard and crystalline. Throughout most of our mountainous regions, subalpine forests clothe the steep mountainsides above the montane forests of the valleys, glacial terraces and moraines.

Although the lowland and montane forests give New Zealand so much of its biological character, most of the former have now gone. The subalpine forests and shrublands, as well as the alpine zone, remain as that part of our natural environment where man has had the least direct impact. But his indirect impact has been considerable through the introduction of wild grazing and browsing animals, particularly deer and goats. The effect of these animals on our indigenous biota has been enormous, particularly in these subalpine forests and shrublands.

◁ WINTER SNOWFALL
An exceptionally heavy snowfall mantles the streambanks and trees of a subalpine beech forest. The weight of such snowfalls can cause considerable damage to the forest; when a branch breaks off, the tree is left exposed to invasion by insect parasites.

SUBALPINE BEECH FOREST
The Travers valley, near its source in Nelson Lakes National Park, cascades between a parkland of snow tussock and scattered small mountain beech trees.

THE SUBALPINE ZONE: Like the lowland and montane forest zones, the subalpine zone decreases in altitude at more southerly latitudes. On the Raukumara Range near East Cape (38°S) the subalpine zone lies between 1,000 m and 1,350 m; on the western slopes of the Tararua Range (41°S) it lies between 900 m and 1,200 m; in northern Fiordland (45°S) the zone has dropped to 600-900 m (Fig. 3, p.152). The upper boundary of the subalpine zone is the sharp transition from continuous woody vegetation to alpine grassland or scattered shrubs and herbs. This 'bushline' or 'timberline' indicates an air-temperature boundary, the altitude above which the shoots of woody plants can no longer grow or ripen. Where beech is the dominant subalpine tree, the transition from stunted forest to alpine grassland is usually quite abrupt. Where beech is absent, a dense, almost impenetrable subalpine shrubland of *Dracophyllum*, the 'leatherwoods' *Olearia* and *Brachyglottis* (formerly *Senecio*) and mountain ribbonwood (*Hoheria lyallii*) occurs. In such regions – the central Westland 'beech gap', Mt Egmont and the ranges north and south of the Manawatu Gorge, for instance – the 'bushline' is not distinct.

On the wetter western (more oceanic) slopes of the Southern Alps, silver beech tends to form the timberline. On the drier eastern (more continental) side of the divide, mountain beech generally dominates the subalpine forests. Here the timberline can be up to 300 m higher than on the western slopes at the same latitude. On the eastern faces of the Richmond Range in Marlborough, for example, the mountain beech timberline is as high as 1,500 m, while across Cook Strait on the west of the southern Tararuas silver beech forms the bushline at 1,200 m. Presumably the warmer, dry summers on the eastern side of the Richmond Range are more favourable for growth than the cool, foggy and windy climate of the Tararuas.

Otherwise, it is difficult to generalise about the 'typical' plants and animals of the subalpine, for it is a transitional zone which varies in nature from place to place throughout our mountains. The brown creeper and the diminutive rifleman, for instance, seem to frequent the subalpine zone in preference to higher and lower altitudes. Other forest birds, such as the tui, silvereye, grey warbler, kaka and parakeet, have a seasonal distribution, preferring the cooler subalpine zone only in the warmer parts of the year. There are a number of key lower-altitude trees, such as kamahi and putaputaweta (*Carpodetus serratus*), that drop out of the forest community at the lower boundary of the subalpine belt. Another important indicator plant is the large tufted fern, *Blechnum discolor*, so common on the floor of montane forest but absent from the subalpine. But many typical montane trees also extend into the subalpine forest. These include silver beech, Hall's totara, and mountain cedar as well as the smaller trees *Pseudopanax colensoi* and *P. simplex*.

Perhaps the most distinctive feature of the subalpine zone is the so-called 'subalpine scrub' just below bushline. This belt of woody shrubs up to 3-4 m in height can be a delight to view from a distance, because of its variety of colour and form compared with the more sombre green of the montane and subalpine forest. But it is the bane of any mountaineer or naturalist attempting to reach the freedom of the alpine herbfields – often on his knees crawling on a slippery carpet of rotting *Olearia* and *Dracophyllum* leaves! Some of the shrubs are really small trees: the beautiful 'tree daisies', *Olearia arborescens*, *O. lacunosa* and *O. ilicifolia*, or the spectacular 'grass tree', *Dracophyllum traversii*. Then there are the 'leatherwoods', such as *Olearia colensoi* which dominates the subalpine shrublands of the northern Tararua and southern Ruahine Ranges. The attractive *Brachyglottis rotundifolius* with its large glossy leaves and cream-coloured flowers held erect on soft, white panicles is a common shrub, as is the leathery-leaved *B. bidwillii*.

Sometimes environmental conditions at low altitudes are sufficiently unfavourable to allow subalpine plants a competitive advantage over typical lowland or montane species. Such conditions often occur in granite country or on old glacial moraines on the western side of the Alps, where the infertile soils are generally either very shallow or waterlogged. Subalpine shrubs, such as *Dracophyllum traversii*, 'pineapple scrub' (*D. menziesii*), inaka (*D. longifolium*), *Archeria traversii*, leatherwood and mountain toatoa, can be found on these sites along with the more characteristic low-fertility vegetation community – shrubs and small trees such as the three attractive podocarps, pink pine (*Dacrydium biforme*), yellow-silver pine (*D. intermedium*) and the extremely slow-growing silver pine (*D. colensoi*).

An interesting example of this 'inversion' of subalpine vegetation occurs where climatic and topographic factors cause pockets of cold air to accumulate at lower altitudes, especially at night. In the Ohikanui valley in the northern Paparoa Range there are 'subalpine' communities at only 200-250 m altitude. Here the lower terraces are dominated by a forest of rimu/mountain cedar/Hall's totara/yellow-silver pine/mountain beech; yet the slopes of the valley (250-500 m) above the terraces are dominated by hard beech, which prefers these higher, yet warmer, sites. Cold air presumably flows down montane valleys like the Ohikanui, Blackwater and Inangahua to discharge into the magnificent lower Buller Gorge. The junction of the Ohikanui and the Buller is only 30 m above sea level, but the vegetation of both valleys at this point is distinctly montane – a mixed red-silver beech forest with some hard beech and kamahi, and rimu emergent above the canopy. But the vegetation of the Buller itself changes dramatically within a kilometre or two, as the cold air meets the mild coastal climate at the mouth of the gorge. Here, on the more fertile soils, tall rimu and kahikatea with northern rata/hinau/kamahi/mahoe make up a true lowland forest with its characteristically luxuriant under-storey. So, within a radius of 5 km, and an altitudinal range of only 200 m, discrete lowland, montane and subalpine vegetational communities can exist.

Similar temperature inversions are known further south in the 'beech gap' forests of central Westland. Here, valleys like the Whitcombe and Hokitika carry the typical podocarp/hardwood forest of rimu, kamahi, southern rata and quintinia. Yet subalpine forest trees like the handsome mountain cedar (*Libocedrus bidwillii*) can occasionally be found at altitudes as low as 300-350 m on more fertile alluvial flats, growing with matai (*Podocarpus spicatus*) or fringing colder flats covered with red tussock (*Chionochloa rubra*).

TWO TRANS-ALPINE JOURNEYS: The presence or absence of beech distinguishes two very different kinds of subalpine forest. Two west to east crossings of the Southern Alps, one in the 'beech gap' of central Westland near Harihari, the other 200 km away, deep in south Westland behind Jackson Bay, serve to illustrate this contrast.

The remaining unlogged forests around Lake Ianthe near Harihari are superb examples of lowland forest containing tall kahikatea and rimu, but as we move across the Alpine Fault the Waitaha, Wanganui or Whataroa Rivers begin to run between sheer, mountainous walls. The forest is montane in character as we travel upstream through kamahi, with scattered emergent southern rata and a subcanopy containing quintinia. Beech trees are entirely absent. The upper reaches of each river are severely gorged, so we would have to climb prominent spurs, leaving kamahi behind us at about 750 m. Probably we would pass through a belt of mountain cedar, their conical crowns standing above the canopy of remaining hardwoods, which have become smaller by now. At around 900 m the fight with the 'subalpine scrub' begins in earnest, but eventually we would emerge, bloody but victorious, in the alpine herbfields. Prolific alpine plant communities would be encountered as we made our way up towards the huge snow névés of the Garden of Eden and Garden of Allah, or perhaps crossed Strachan Pass or Perth Col to descend to the headwaters of the great Canterbury rivers, the Rakaia and the Rangitata. On the drier eastern side, beech is still absent and the subalpine scrub lacks many of the western species. The problem of descending through this subalpine scrub is sometimes solved by rolling down on top of its tight canopy! This subalpine forest is not so distinct from the shrubland, for there are now many shrubby trees, such as fuchsia (*Fuchsia excorticata*), ribbonwood (*Hoheria lyallii*) and the smaller-leaved kowhai (*Sophora microphylla*). Broadleaf (*Griselinia littoralis*) sometimes forms a canopy occasionally pierced by Hall's totara.

BLUE LAKE
At the head of the West Sabine River, Blue Lake nestles at the foot of a moraine wall. The tussock-covered fan contrasts with the mountain beech on the older, more stable surfaces.

In south Westland, by way of contrast, beech completely dominates the forests. Travel up the magnificent broad glaciated sweep of the Arawata is much easier. The lowland rimu/rata/kamahi forest near the coast soon gives way to silver beech but this changes dramatically, and rather inexplicably, to red beech near the junction with the Waipara. From here on, up through Ten Hour Gorge and the upper gorges of the Arawata, red beech dominates the forest until, within 200 m of bushline, silver beech once again becomes dominant. This is a reversal on a grand scale, since red beech generally prefers warmer, more fertile sites. Perhaps this red beech is a relict population, by-passed by the more aggressive silver beech which colonised the floor of the lower valley after the retreat of the Arawata Glaciers. In the head of the Arawata above the subalpine silver beech there is a belt of 'subalpine scrub', but it is much narrower on the sides of the valley. After crossing Arawata Saddle on the Barrier Range the 'scrub' belt is almost non-existent. Silver beech again predominates in this subalpine forest, but further to the east in the drier valleys of the Dart and Matukituki mountain beech is the dominant subalpine species. As we travel out of the mountains along the floor of the Dart or West Matukituki, red beech again reappears, to dominate the lower reaches of each valley with magnificent trees up to 150 cm in diameter and 30 m in height.

SNOW TOTARA
Snow totara, Podocarpus nivalis, *is a semi-prostrate shrub commonly found in subalpine shrublands and low-alpine herbfields. Like the lower-altitude totaras, the snow totara is distributed by birds which eat the ripe seeds and their brightly coloured, fleshy receptacles.*

Here in the drier montane valley floors of north-west Otago, red beech dominates, but north of the 'beech gap', in the Waimakariri valley of Canterbury, it is mountain beech that dominates – not only the montane forest but also the entire subalpine zone as a pure forest stand all the way to bushline at around 1,400 m. Both forests have their attractions – dappled patterns of light, for example, and ease of travel through lack of under-storey plants. It was once possible to find the brilliant red, parasitic mistletoe (*Peraxilla tetrapetala*) adorning trees in both Otago and Canterbury beech forests. Sadly, it is now becoming rare through the browsing of possums.

To summarise then, the nature and distribution of subalpine forest and shrublands is dynamic. They depend upon historical events like the Pleistocene glaciations, which swept beech from the central part of the Southern Alps; or the volcanic eruptions of long ago that may have eliminated beech from the forests of Mt Egmont. Subtle topographic/climatic effects like aspect or the drainage of cold air into mountain basins also determine the location of typical 'subalpine' communities. Low soil fertility may lead to subalpine communities on some sites at low altitudes. In addition, burning has caused some subalpine forests on the drier, eastern side of the Southern Alps to be replaced by tussock grasslands.

Finally, subalpine vegetation communities on Stewart Island are so different from all others that they fall into a category of their own. Snow is rare or unknown and wind is a dominant environmental factor. Not only is beech absent, but a whole host of other subalpine trees and shrubs – including mountain toatoa, mountain cedar and kowhai – are not present. There may be as many as 20 plants endemic to Stewart Island, and most of these are restricted to the open, subalpine vegetation. Rimu appears to have a very wide ecological range and appears to be present in all size classes: this is most unusual on the main islands of New Zealand. These shrublands are bleak and inhospitable, but they demonstrate again the resilience of the woody members of our flora in adapting to the wet, cold, windy, steep, and unstable subalpine environment.

△ BEECH SAPLINGS
Sunlight filters through beech forest to a floor cleared of undergrowth by wild introduced animals, particularly deer and goats. Now, after years of deer hunting, beech seedlings are regenerating profusely in some areas. Animal numbers have been controlled in recent years by helicopter hunting on the alpine grasslands. However, there are now indications that deer are responding to this pressure by spending more time in the shelter of the subalpine forests – the forests of critical importance for the protection of steep mountain slopes.

◁ TRAVERS RIVER, NELSON LAKES NATIONAL PARK
Beech forest clothes the sides of steep river valleys around the beautiful Nelson lakes, Rotoiti and Rotoroa. Here, a typical forest rises from the river to the bushline at approximately 1,400 m, where it ceases abruptly, giving way to snow tussock and herbfield. Both silver and mountain beech are found in this forest, but mountain beech is dominant at the bushline. The park-like effect has been enhanced by grazing of the small flats by deer.

◁ BLUE LAKE, NELSON LAKES NATIONAL PARK
Perched behind an old glacial moraine, Blue Lake is fed by an underground river, which flows from the alpine Lake Constance. From the outlet of Blue Lake, the West Sabine River cascades in a series of sparkling falls down the old moraine face, now clothed with mountain beech and lacebark.

RAOULIA, ALGAE AND STONES ▷
At higher altitudes conditions become less favourable for growth. Yet here, in a dry riverbed, a mat of raoulia has developed among boulders colonised by red algae. Different species of raoulia form small patches among rocks and gravel in the subalpine zone in most mountainous areas.

△
WEST SABINE TARN
The imprint of past glaciation is still to be seen on the valley floor where these tarns fill shallow depressions. The tarns are rimmed with a thick bed of *Sphagnum* moss.

MOUNTAIN LACEBARK, ▷
Hoheria lyallii
When the mountain lacebark flowers in February, its large leaves and white blossoms contrast dramatically with the much smaller and more sombre foliage of the mountain beech.

△
Brachyglottis rotundifolius
This 'leatherwood' was until recently called *Senecio reinoldii*. A small tree that is common on the coast, it will sometimes be found, along with species of *Olearia* and *Dracophyllum*, in place of beech at the bushline. Clumps of these shrubs form a dense scrub that is almost impenetrable. These plants, photographed near the upper limits of mountain beech forests in Fiordland were 3-4 m tall.

SUBALPINE FOREST ▷
Mountain beech and kaikawaka mingle to form an open-canopied forest at 1,000 m on the western slopes of Mt Ruapehu. Subalpine forests at this altitude are frequently swathed in heavy mists or drenched with rain, and at times covered in snow. The thick undergrowth includes mountain toatoa, coprosmas, astelias, mountain cabbage tree and umbrella fern, while the beech trunks often support lichen gardens.

◁ HOLLYFORD RIVER, FIORDLAND
The Hollyford River passes through silver beech forest in its upper reaches in the heavily glaciated Darran Mountains. One of the great rivers of Fiordland, the Hollyford eventually flows north into Lake McKerrow and Martins Bay on the West Coast.

△
WILMOT PASS, FIORDLAND
New fronds of blechnum fern abound in this clearing in the rain-drenched forest surrounding the Wilmot Pass. Lichens and mosses festoon the trees.

HAKEKE, *Olearia ilicifolia*
Hakeke is a member of the large genus *Olearia* that has at least 32 species in New Zealand. It is a feature of the scrub found towards the bushline in the subalpine zone, but also grows on the edge of the forest at lower altitudes. A shrub or tree that can grow to 6-7m, it is often called mountain holly, presumably because of the spiky leaf margins. Hakeke is found in many parts of the country south of East Cape.
▽

SPANIARD, *Aciphylla horrida* ▷
Bearing pointed leaves up to 15 cm long, this large and colourful spaniard grows in the wetter parts along the main divide of the South Island, particulary in Otago and Fiordland. Its habitat is primarily subalpine scrub, where it mingles with coprosmas, hebes, olearias and other plants.

STREAMSIDE, FIORDLAND
As the montane forest gives way to subalpine forest and shrubland, flowering shrubs and herbs, such as hebe, ranunculus, and the yellow-flowered composite (*Dolichoglottis lyallii*) shown here, can be found bordering the cold streams that fall from the alpine regions.

△
NATURAL SUBALPINE GARDENS
There is a great variety of texture and shape amongst subalpine foliage. Here in Fiordland, *Dracophyllum menziesii* with its long curving leaves, contrasts with the branchlets of coprosma. Each subalpine plant has evolved its own defences against the weight of winter snow.

PYGMY PINE, *Dacrydium laxifolium*
This plant, the world's smallest pine, grows as a prostrate shrub in the New Zealand subalpine zone. It is found in poorly drained and boggy sites with plenty of light, particularly from the Tongariro volcanoes southwards.

◁ INAKA, *Dracophyllum longifolium*
This shrub, usually growing to 2-3 m tall in the subalpine zone, is one of the most widespread members of the genus *Dracophyllum*. It is very common in the high rainfall areas of the South Island and Stewart Island and likes habitats as various as the margin of the coastal forest in Fiordland and the bushline in the same region. It is also frequently found in the uplands of eastern Otago, where it tends to invade the tussock grasslands on the wetter, peaty sites.

TAKAHE, *Notornis mantelli* ▷
Once living in both North and South Islands, this large flightless rail was considered extinct until it was discovered in 1948 in the subalpine region of the Murchison Mountains in Fiordland. Even in this last retreat the number of birds is dropping steadily, as they compete with deer for available food and are preyed on by stoats. The takahe feed largely off the bases of tussocks, and so, in the only instance of agricultural practice in a national park, fertiliser is being applied to the tussock in an effort to help the bird in its struggle for survival.

△
Brachyglottis bidwillii
At higher altitudes in the alpine and subalpine zones, this plant reaches only 20-30 cm; further down it grows as a low, branching shrub. The thick leaves and springy foliage enable it to survive the winter snow. It is another species recently transferred from the genus *Senecio*.

△
MOUNTAIN FLAX, *Phormium cookianum*
Although it will grow at sea level in some places, as around Cook Strait, this flax prefers poorly drained, peaty sites usually near the bushline. It is smaller than the more common New Zealand flax, *P. tenax*. Flowers seem to vary in colour from one mountain range to another. These were photographed in the Tararua Range.

Coprosma ciliata
This low shrub, growing from lowland to the upper reaches of subalpine shrubland, is found in North, South and Stewart Islands.
▽

BEECH, LICHEN, SNOW ▷
As the snow falls it accumulates in the crowns of the mountain beech trees. These dead branches encrusted with lichen gradually snap off under the weight of snow.

△
MOUNTAIN BEECH
Plants in the subalpine vegetation belt must be able to withstand periodic winter snowfalls. These stunted mountain beech trees have survived many heavy snowfalls like this one. Smaller shrubs, herbs and grasses will remain buried sometimes for several weeks until rains thaw the snow.

△
ICED TWIGS
When strong, moisture-laden winds lash the subalpine zone, a thick layer of ice, rather than snow, will sometimes cover the twigs of the trees.

◁ FROST HEAVE
At higher altitudes in the mountainous regions the phenomenon known as 'frost heave' can be seen. If mineral soil is exposed by the removal of the overlying vegetation and humus layers, the very cold temperatures overnight can force water from the ground as thin ice needles. These needles are sometimes capped with soil or small stones and, as they thaw during the hotter part of the day, the top layer of soil is loosened and becomes very susceptible to erosion by wind and water.

SUBALPINE ZONE, MT RUAPEHU
Here, on the subalpine slopes of Mt Ruapehu, mountain beech still hangs on tenuously as the soft soil from volcanic ash is gradually eroded on all sides. These isolated pedestals of vegetation are a common feature of the subalpine zone particularly on the western slopes of the mountain.

CHAPTER EIGHT

Alpine Gardens

Mountains are New Zealand's most dramatic landforms. The magnificent Southern Alps tower up to 3,700m above sea level in the Mt Cook region and there is a virtually continuous chain of mountains, 2,000-2,500m high, from Milford Sound in Fiordland to the Kaikoura Ranges in Marlborough. But this is only the main divide; in addition there are probably more than a hundred subsidiary mountain ranges rising to at least 1,200m. The mountains of the North Island are the isolated volcanic massifs of Taranaki and Tongariro and the more modest northern equivalent of the Alps – the axial ranges (Tararua, Ruahine, Kaimanawa-Kaweka, Huiarau and Raukumara) that extend from Wellington to East Cape.

The lower limit of the alpine zone is the 'bushline' and the upper limit the summer snow line (the height to which snow thaws during most summers). Figure 3 (p. 152) shows that the alpine zone also decreases in altitude towards more southerly latitudes. On the Raukumara Range the bushline occurs at around 1,500m, steadily decreasing to around 900m in Fiordland. On Mt Ruapehu the upper limit of the alpine zone is about 2,400m decreasing to around 2,000m in Fiordland. Consequently, the alpine zone can be very wide, a vertical height of as much as 1,000m on the higher mountains, such as the Kaikoura Ranges and the Canterbury and Otago Alps. Above this summer snow level lies the harsh nival zone of permanent snow and ice where only lichens and a few very hardy flowering plants of genera such as *Ranunculus, Parahebe, Haastia, Hebe* and *Epilobium* can survive on snow free rocks and crevices. In subalpine regions of the drier, cold mountains of Central Otago, the forest has long since been replaced by tussock grasses and so no bushline marks the beginning of the alpine zone. Here, the common hard tussock, *Festuca novae-zelandiae* acts as a useful indicator, for its upper limit is about the same as that formerly reached by the subalpine forest.

The stark grandeur of our alpine scenery – precipices and cirques, snowfields and icefalls – is softened in summer by the profusion of flowering alpine plants, a joy to mountaineer and botanist alike. The bleak mountain slopes of winter are transformed into alpine gardens, with many of the plants adapting ingeniously in order to survive in this very harsh environment. The 600 or so higher plant species that grow above the bushline make up about 30 per cent of New Zealand's total flora of higher plants (that is, plants other than lichens, mosses, liverworts and algae). This is a large proportion for such a climatically severe environment; even more remarkable is the fact that 93 per cent of this alpine flora is endemic to the New Zealand biological region, compared with 80 per cent for all higher plant species. (See Table 1, p. 13.) This level of endemism might seem to indicate that the alpine flora is of considerable antiquity and has gradually evolved within this alpine environment to exploit the wide variety of ecological niches available – screes, cliffs, cirques, bogs and tarns, moraine-fields, stream levees, glacial and stream terraces as well as snowbanks. Yet the most recent phase of mountain-building did not begin until around 5 million years ago and the alpine zone probably was not extensive until the onset of the Pleistocene Ice Ages around 2 million years ago. This is a very short time compared with the 50-100 million years or more that elements of our kauri, podocarp and beech forests have been present at lower altitudes. This enigma has stimulated a considerable amount of scientific debate and we will return to it after taking a closer look at the different alpine plant communities as they exist today.

LOW ALPINE VEGETATION: The term 'low alpine' refers to the lower 300-500m of the alpine zone, not to the vegetation itself which is considerably taller (up to 1.5m) than the shorter cushion plant communities (up to 30cm) found in the 'high alpine zone'. Immediately above bushline is the snow tussock/herbfield or a mixed snow tussock/shrubland, where the subalpine shrubs (Chapter 7) mingle with shrubs such as snow totara (*Podocarpus nivalis*), hebes, and coprosmas such as *C. pseudocuneata* and *C. depressa.* More alpine members of the amazing genus *Dracophyllum* also make their appearance: *Dracophyllum kirkii* in the wetter western slopes of the Southern Alps, the

◁ TEMPLE BASIN
Screes of greywacke rock pour from the peaks at the head of Temple Basin above Arthur's Pass in the Southern Alps. Even in this inhospitable alpine environment, alpine herbs and grasses have managed to survive, especially on the more stable parts of the landscape.

OTAGO ALPS
Mountains have always had an irresistible attraction for explorers. The Humboldt Mountains, the Barrier Range and the Mt Earnslaw massif at the head of Lake Wakatipu have drawn many European explorers and, before them, Polynesians in search of greenstone.

distinctive rich, rusty-brown *D. recurvum* on the summits of the Kaimanawa Mountains, or the attractive blue-green gleam of *D. pubescens* so characteristic of this tussock/shrubland in the mountains of north-west Nelson.

The dominant plants of this low alpine zone are the snow tussocks. They occur throughout the mountain chain from Hikurangi in the Raukumara Range to Fiordland, as well as on Mt Anglem at the northern end of Stewart Island. The most widespread species is mid-ribbed snow tussock (*Chionochloa pallens*), which seems to prefer the better-drained, more fertile soils in this environment. In the Tararua Range it is joined by a broad-leaved snow tussock (*C. flavescens*) which occupies the less fertile and poorly-drained sites. In the South Island, another broad-leaved snow tussock with strap-like leaves (as yet unnamed) occurs with *C. pallens*. This species also occupies fertile, well-drained sites and is especially important in limestone areas such as the Matiri Range and parts of north-west Nelson. The hardier *C. crassiuscula*, with its distinctive tangle of curled-up dead blade ends, gradually replaces these species at higher altitudes while the glistening *C. teretifolia* (a beautiful sight when it occasionally forms seedheads) takes over on the peaty soils of southern Fiordland. One of the most attractive of the *Chionochloa* species is 'carpet grass', *C. australis*, which forms extensive areas of an extremely dense and compact turf in both the low alpine and higher alpine zone of the north-western South Island, from the Tasman Mountains to the Spenser Mountains and Lewis Pass region.

HIMALAYAN THAR
The thar, Hemitragus jemlahicus, *was successfully introduced as a game animal in 1904 and again in 1909 to the Mt Cook region. Equally at home in the Southern Alps or their Himalayan homeland, these alpine goats are superbly adapted for travel at high altitudes. Unfortunately, their browsing severely damages alpine vegetation.*

Throughout this alpine grassland, herbs shelter between the tussocks, in rock crevices or in the lee of rock outcrops. These communities of alpine buttercups (*Ranunculus*), daisies (*Celmisia*), gentians, the speargrasses or spaniards (*Aciphylla*) and anisotomes of the carrot family, and the white-flowered ourisias with their attractive, often large, glossy leaves – all add colour and variety to this snow tussock/herbfield. Sadly, so many of these palatable herbs (such as *Ranunculus* and *Ourisia*) as well as the tussocks, have been selectively grazed by red deer, chamois and thar. In many areas the floristic diversity has gone, leaving an alpine herbfield dominated by less palatable species of *Celmisia* and *Aciphylla*.

HIGH ALPINE VEGETATION: Gradually, the snow tussock/herbfield gives way to the more stunted high alpine plant communities, ('fellfield'). In the greywacke and schist mountains, stable boulderfields or 'dry fellfields' are common. Here, small spaniards such as *Aciphylla dobsonii* and *A. simplex* can be found along with one of the most amazing growth forms in the alpine zone – the 'vegetable sheep' (species of *Raoulia* and *Haastia*) that form cushions up to 2 m in diameter. On inaccessible rocky ledges we may be lucky enough to find one or more species of silvery-leaved edelweiss (*Leucogenes leontopodium, L. grandiceps* and two other unnamed species), surely some of the most beautiful of our alpine plants. The drier rocky fellfields harbour many other interesting plants: *Hectorella caespitosa*, a remarkable cushion plant when in flower, and other cushion plants of the genus *Chionohebe*; *Pachycladon novae-zelandiae*, a feature of exposed sites on the schist mountains, where its strong taproot helps it to resist frost heave; and the deep-green cushions of *Phyllachne colensoi*, which colonises an extraordinary variety of sites – snow hollows, exposed ridges and detritus traps between rocks.

In the wetter fellfields or around mountain streams two species of *Celmisia, C. sessiliflora* and *C. bellidioides*, both form attractive flowering mats. In Fiordland, and the wetter parts of Otago and south Westland, one of the most striking herbs in wet fellfield, *Aciphylla congesta* (with its white 'cauliflower-like' flower head), is often found growing in association with the smallest of the *Chionochloa* species, *C. oreophila* (snow-patch grass).

Screes are among the most inhospitable habitats in the high alpine zone. These huge piles of angular stones usually slope at an angle of over 30° and are particularly characteristic of the greywacke mountains from Marlborough to north Otago. There are about 25 alpine plant species confined to screes (as distinct from stable boulderfields). Most have specialised features to conserve moisture or withstand movement; these include taproots or rhizomes, succulent and waxy leaves, and the ability to shed their leaves easily. A common plant is *Ranunculus haastii*, its blue-grey leaves making it virtually indistinguishable from the surrounding greywacke debris, until it produces its bright yellow flowers. Two members of the *Cotula* genus, *C. dendyi* and *C. atrata*, brighten the scree slopes with their large yellow and black, button-like flower heads. The penwiper plant, *Notothlaspi rosulatum* (so called because of its rosette of many grey, felty leaves), must surely count as one of the most attractive scree plants of our drier, greywacke mountains.

The severity of the alpine scree environment is matched on the broad, plateau summits of the higher, relatively dry, 'rain-shadow' mountains of Central Otago – the Pisa and Old Man Ranges and the Dunstan and Garvie Mountains. Daily extremes of temperature (including freezing and thawing) and strong winds mean that the vegetation is reduced to extremely dwarfed, cushion plants, in many ways resembling the tundra of the Arctic. Yet, even in this the harshest of our high alpine environments many plants have found a habitat – most of them in the 'rippled landscape' of patterned ground so characteristic of this landscape. These features – solifluction terraces, soil hummocks and soil stripes – are relict features, visible imprints on the land of the freeze-thaw climate prevailing as the ice sheets retreated from these mountain summits thousands of years ago. Here the smallest of our many *Dracophyllum* species, *D. muscoides*, tends to dominate as a cushion plant, often with silver-green mats of *Raoulia hectori* and the occasional tuft of slim snow grass, *Chionochloa macra*, which was probably more common before fires ravaged the fragile vegetation of these summits.

KEA
These large and attractive parrots, Nestor notabilis, *are confined to the high country of the South Island. They generally nest in the subalpine beech forest, but forage widely in the alpine zone, eating primarily vegetation and insects. Their curiosity and amusing antics have earned them the affection of all who have observed them in their natural habitat. They are truly the court jesters of the alpine realm.*

THE ORIGINS OF OUR ALPINE FLORA AND FAUNA: The large numbers of plant species endemic to the alpine zone have been considered recent in origin because New Zealand's mountains are relatively young. This view is supported by the lack of any ancient fossil records of our alpine plant genera. As many common alpine plant genera are also found at lower altitudes (for example, *Celmisia, Hebe, Dracophyllum, Coprosma, Aciphylla*), it is easy to imagine that these evolved species suited to the new alpine environment. This is also thought to be the mode of origin for the mountain parrot, the kea, which probably evolved during the Pleistocene Age in the cold South Island from the main *Nestor* stock, the forest-dwelling kaka. Similarly, the diminutive rock wren evolved from the forest-dwelling bush wren, which, rather ironically, is probably now extinct. Alpine wetas, cicadas and other insects probably had similar origins. A more radical variant of this theory suggests that most of our alpine plant genera were derived from the northern hemisphere, and reached the newly formed mountains of New Zealand via the mountains of South East Asia and Australia, or as seeds or spores on migratory birds, in the last 3 million years or so.

However, some of the high alpine genera are very distinctive taxonomically: *Hectorella* (only one species, in a family of its own); or the scree boulderfield genera endemic to New Zealand (*Lignocarpa, Pachycladon, Notothlaspi*) which, because of their highly specialised organs, could well be a more ancient part of the flora. All these genera have only one or very few species, as do a number of other endemic alpine genera (*Leucogenes, Chionohebe* and *Haastia*). A number of our other alpine genera (*Forstera, Donatia, Phyllachne, Rostkovia*) contain very few species and are also represented in other southern Gondwanaland fragments – Australia, New Guinea, South America or the subantarctic islands. There is a strong case for suggesting that most of this group evolved within New Zealand or invaded from Antarctica by a land bridge or 'island-hopping'.

In this case the lower alpine zone members of the above group, and other subalpine plants, such as the more primitive podocarps snow totara (*Podocarpus nivalis*) and pigmy pine (*Dacrydium laxifolium*) and mountain toatoa (*Phyllocladus asplenifolius* variety *alpinus*), would be the remnants of a Tertiary age 'alpine flora'. These plants may have survived this warmer epoch on cooler upland peneplains with very infertile soils almost continually leached by rain. Environmental conditions like these occur today at low altitudes in parts of Westland, Fiordland and Stewart Island and it is not hard to see why some of the more primitive *Dacrydium* species (*D. intermedium* and *D. colensoi*, for example) predominate on these infertile soils rather than in the higher, steeper parts of the Southern Alps, where soils are being rejuvenated by the drift downslope of debris and soluble nutrients.

AN ALPINE GARDEN
The beauty of the alpine flower gardens in springtime and summer complements the grandeur of the alpine scenery. Here edelweiss, Leucogenes grandiceps, *flourishes.*

Whatever the origins of New Zealand's alpine flora, it is one of the outstanding biological features of the country. Despite the past ravages of wild introduced animals there are signs in recent times that animal population control has led to a resurgence of flowering herbs and grasses in our mountain lands. Here, the ancient and the more adaptive and opportunistic species intermingle, at times with a dazzling beauty that quite eclipses any effort of man to create botanic gardens.

CRAIGIEBURN RANGE, CANTERBURY
The Craigieburn Range lies 50 km to the east of the Southern Alps and falls within their 'rain shadow'. A sharp bushline of mountain beech gives way to a snow tussock/shrubland in the low alpine zone. Much of this region was burnt and overgrazed in the past, and the greywacke mountain slopes show typical signs of accelerated erosion, although the higher screes are natural features that have probably never been covered in vegetation.

SNOW TUSSOCK/SHRUBLAND ▷
Seedheads of mid-ribbed snow tussock (*Chionochloa pallens*) glint in the sunlight on the slopes above Arthur's Pass. This is a typical low alpine snow tussock/shrubland community, the dominant shrub being the common 'turpentine shrub', *Dracophyllum uniflorum*, which shows its characteristic summer yellow-brown in this photograph. Most of the *Celmisia* species and other herbs have finished flowering but the community is still colourful.

◁ MOUNTAIN RIDGES
The summit ridges of the Tararua Range are a good example of a low alpine snow tussock community. Here broad-leaved snow tussock (*Chionochloa flavescens*) predominates on the poorly drained hollows and mid-ribbed snow tussock (*C. pallens*) on the better drained slopes. The underlying rocks are greywacke, and the landscape has been strongly influenced by faulting.

Celmisia semicordata
This is the largest of the 50 or so species of *Celmisia* in the alpine zone. Formerly known as *C. coriacea*, this beautiful plant is quite common in snow tussock/herbfield in the high rainfall regions south of Nelson. Flowers can be up to 10 cm in diameter and clumps of the plant as large as 2 m.

△
MT EARNSLAW
The west (*left*) and east (*right*) peaks of Mt Earnslaw on the Forbes Mountains are framed against a backdrop of the Otago section of the main divide – here called the Barrier Range. Both mountain ranges are part of Mt Aspiring National Park. Here the rocks are schists, and the extensive screes seen on the greywacke mountains of Canterbury are less evident. Whereas deer have caused the deterioration of the low alpine snow tussock grasslands in Mt Aspiring National Park, these tussock slopes have been periodically grazed by sheep for many years.

MOUNTAIN HAREBELL, *Wahlenbergia albomarginata*
Widespread from the coast to the low alpine zone, clumps of these pretty harebells grow in open places such as snow tussock/herbfield.

MOUNTAIN CASCADE
Water splashed from a cascading mountain stream can maintain a damp environment ideal for a number of alpine plants – *Geum uniflorum* or species of *Ranunculus*, *Caltha* or *Euphrasia*.

Ranunculus insignis ▷
Ranunculus insignis is one of the more widespread alpine buttercups, from the Raukumara Range in the north to mid-Canterbury in the south. It can stand up to 60 cm high in favourable sites along stream banks with its glossy-petalled flowers up to 5 cm in diameter. Although not as tall as the magnificent white-flowered great mountain buttercup (*R. lyallii*), it is still claimed to be one of the largest buttercups in the world.

◁ ANGELUS TARN
Mountain tarns, filling old glacial hollows, are a feature of most alpine regions. Here, at the southern end of the Robert Ridge above Lake Rotoiti, Angelus Tarn nestles in a basin. Mid-ribbed snowgrass (*Chionochloa pallens*) dominates the tussock landscape but many moisture-loving plants, such as species of *Drosera*, thrive around the edge of the tarn.

UPPER OTIRA RIVER
The headwaters of the Otira lie high in the fellfields under the north-western slopes of Mt Rolleston in the Southern Alps. On its turbulent way to the montane forest of rata and Hall's totara in the upper Otira Gorge, the stream passes through snow tussock/herbfield and a subalpine belt of leatherwood, neinei (*Dracophyllum traversii*), mountain cedar and pink pine (*Dacrydium biforme*).
▽

Drosera arcturi
Alpine sundews such as *Drosera arcturi* are often found in boggy places and around the edges of lakes and tarns, not only in alpine regions but also down to the montane zone. Attractive and colourful plants, they have tiny hairs each with a sticky globule which traps small insects. These are gradually absorbed by the plant.

BLUE DUCK, *Hymenolaimus malacorhynchos*
Pairs of these handsome birds are often found foraging for aquatic insects in the rapids of larger alpine streams during summer, although they also inhabit streams in montane and subalpine forests. The blue duck is an endemic bird of exceptional interest, as it has no close relatives anywhere else in the world. The male emits a characteristic whistle which is the origin of the bird's Maori name – whio.

△
SOUTH ISLAND EDELWEISS, *Leucogenes grandiceps*
The South Island edelweiss is one of four species of native edelweiss, all of them found in the alpine zone. The New Zealand edelweiss should not be confused with the famous European edelweiss (*Leontopodium alpinum*). The New Zealand edelweiss is usually conspicuous because its preferred habitats are exposed rock outcrops or dry fellfields where it shelters in rock crevices. With its soft, silvery leaves and charming flowers it is a sight to excite any visitor to the higher mountain regions.

VEGETABLE SHEEP, *Haastia pulvinaris*
'Vegetable sheep', *Haastia pulvinaris*, are common in the dry fellfields of the Kaikoura Range and the Spenser Mountains. They seem to prefer the stable boulderfield that accumulates from shattered greywacke, and can not survive on mobile screes. Their yellow flowers can give the impression that brightly dyed fleeces, up to 2 m across, have been laid out to dry on the rock outcrops. Further south in Canterbury greyish-white cushions of two other 'vegetable sheep', *Raoulia mammillaris* and *R. maxima*, often decorate the rocky fellfields.

Previous page
WINTER SNOWS, MT RUAPEHU

△
ROCKY BENCH
A boulderfield at the foot of rocky outcrops above Temple Basin near Arthur's Pass is a typical habitat for some dry fellfield plants – small spaniards, species of *Raoulia* and *Haastia*, or many small species of *Celmisia*, such as the silvery carpets of *Celmisia incana*, or *C. laricifolia* with its creeping stems forming low mats among the boulders.

Hebe Haastii
Hebe haastii is one of the hardiest of alpine shrubs for it extends from 1,200 m right up into the nival zone at 2,900 m. With *Parahebe birleyi* it shares the honour of the highest recorded elevation for a vascular plant in New Zealand. Its preferred habitats are crevices in rocky fellfield (as shown) or screes.

HANGING VALLEY ▷
Under the slopes of Mt Rolleston the upper Otira issues from a hanging valley filled with screes. But the sides of the valley contain more stable sites where flowering plants – edelweiss, *Pratia*, *Celmisia* and *Euphrasia* – can be found.

◁ SCREE SLOPES
This photograph shows scree accumulation on the flanks of rocky peaks near Arthur's Pass. The fresh grey colour of the screes is typical of greywacke country. In places the screes can be seen perched above more stable fellfield communities that show up with their yellow and pale green colours. Screes are among the most inhospitable habitats in the high alpine zone. Plants colonising screes have to be able to withstand the movement, and lack of moisture, in the upper layer of stones. Some screes are entirely devoid of scree plants, usually where the scree is very recent or the depth to underlying soil is too great for plants to reach with their roots.

◁ *Anisotome pilifera*
This herb is very typical of the dry fellfield, growing particularly on rocky ledges and crevices or bluffs. It was once widespread throughout most of the higher mountain regions of the South Island, but in many areas it has been eliminated from all but the most inaccessible sites because it is so palatable to introduced animals.

△
SCREE PLANTS
Two common scree plants, the yellow-flowered *Cotula pyrethrifolia* and the reddish-brown willow herb *Epilobium glabellum*, have colonised this greywacke scree. Despite the mobility of this substratum and the obvious restrictions on moisture and nutrient supply, these and at least 20 or so other species of alpine plants have evolved to live in this severe environment.

STONEFIELD DAISY, *Haastia sinclairii*
Haastia sinclairii is another plant of the dry fellfield, which also grows sometimes on scree. It is an attractive, trailing plant up to 30 cm long with felty whitish leaves. It is restricted to the South Island and can be found up to an altitude of 2,000 m.

△
SUMMIT OF OLD MAN RANGE
The summits of the higher, relatively dry, 'rain-shadow' mountains of Central Otago – the Pisa and Old Man Ranges and Garvie and Dunstan Mountains – are among the harshest alpine environments in New Zealand. Wind blows almost constantly and in many places the former vegetation of slim snow tussock (*Chionochloa macra*) has been stripped away. The schist tors, standing above the surface like ancient obelisks, provide the only protection for plants. In these climatic extremes, where the earth may be frozen for up to six months of the year and the average daily windrun may be a phenomenal 450 km, the surviving vegetation is reduced to dwarfed cushion plants somewhat resembling the tundra of the Arctic.

SOUTH ISLAND PIED OYSTERCATCHER, *Haematopus ostralegus finschi*
These birds breed in the river beds and lake shores of the tussock country of the South Island. Here, on the Old Man Range, they breed in the alpine herbfield below the summit of the range. It is not uncommon for them to 'dive-bomb' human intruders in an attempt to drive them away. In the winter they migrate to estuaries and harbours, particularly those of the north.

△
EROSION PAVEMENT, OLD MAN RANGE
The summits of the higher Central Otago mountains show an amazing variety of surface patterns. Here, on the Old Man Range, flat slabs of schist rock form a pavement where the soil has been eroded by the wind. There are also furrows, termed 'soil stripes', which are relict features, visible imprints of the severe freeze-thaw climate prevailing as the ice sheets retreated from these mountain summits thousands of years ago. Yet a few cushion plants can survive here. These include *Dracophyllum muscoides* (the smallest member of the widespread *Dracophyllum* genus) which can easily be mistaken for a patch of moss since its leaves are only 2-3 mm long. In less exposed situations, another important cushion plant, *Raoulia hectori*, forms silvery mats up to 1 m in size.

Hebe buchananii ▷
Hebe buchananii can often be found in the drier mountains of the South Island, its stout branches, with the characteristic hebe leaf arrangement, tentatively reaching out of crevices in highly exposed sites in rocky fellfields.

ALPINE GENTIAN
Gentians are among the most attractive alpine plants. Virtually all of New Zealand's 19 species of gentian can be found in the alpine zone but many are very localised and there is an element of taxonomic confusion which makes identification of many plants difficult. Gentians are among the last of the alpine plants to flower, some as late as April.
▽

CUSHION/HERBFIELD, OLD MAN RANGE
On the lee slopes of the Old Man Range the wind is considerably reduced and a number of taller herbs, such as *Celmisia viscosa* and *C. haastii*, will grow along with many cushion plants that tend to cover the soil stripes, hummocks and other varieties of patterned ground. Further down the slope where the slope angle increases, the landscape takes on a more 'rippled' look because of the predominance of other features like 'solifluction terraces', old earth flows formed through prolonged freezing and thawing of the wet ground as the ice sheets retreated.

Celmisia sessiliflora
Celmisia sessiliflora is very common on permanently damp sites in the snow tussock/herbfields of the South Island and Stewart Island. It is easily recognised by its greenish-grey colour and its dense cushion habit. The flowers are quite large (about 4 cm) and, unlike most *Celmisia* species, are on short stalks so that the plant can look like a most attractive flower carpet up to 1 m wide. It has a wide altitudinal range and habitats include wet fellfield, bogs and snowbanks – in fact most sheltered, moist sites.

CHAPTER NINE

The Volcanic Lands

If the South Island is celebrated for its mountain grandeur, the North Island is equally known, here and abroad, for its volcanic landscapes. In the South Island the only volcanoes, barely recognisable as such, are Banks and Otago Peninsulas; but the North Island has four major volcanic centres: the immense Taupo Volcanic Zone stretching 250 km from the continuously active volcano of White Island in the Bay of Plenty to Mt Ruapehu; the Taranaki Volcanic Zone dominated by the dormant volcano Mt Egmont; and the lesser volcanic zones of Auckland and the Bay of Islands. The North Island is also dotted with other extinct volcanoes, including Pirongia, Karioi and Mangatautari in the Waikato and the recently active Mayor Island off Waihi.

To understand why volcanic features are so prominent in the North Island landscape, we must return to the concept of 'plate tectonics' introduced in Chapter 1. The outermost 60 km or so of the earth consists of solid rock (crust and upper mantle), which is divided into eight major plates. These plates are jostled about by convection currents in the semi-fluid mantle far beneath. The continents ride as passengers on these plates and cannot be destroyed because they consist of lighter rocks (such as granite) than those of the ocean floor (basalt). The ocean floor basalts are continually being created by an upwelling of lava at sea floor ridges. The lava spreads in two directions, thereby contributing to the formation of the two adjacent plates. As these plates are forced apart, they collide with other plates; one of them then dips (usually the denser, thinner ocean floor plate) and its material re-enters the earth's interior at a steep angle. This is called a 'subduction zone' and is usually marked by a deep ocean trench. In simple terms, the system can be thought of as a huge conveyor-belt of crust moving outwards from ocean floor ridges.

As one plate collides with another, earthquakes and volcanoes occur, particularly in the so-called 'ring of fire' around the huge Pacific Plate. New Zealand sits astride the junction of two plates – the Pacific Plate and the Indian-Australian Plate. However, this junction is very complicated. In the North Island off the east coast, the Pacific Plate is being pushed under the Indian-Australian Plate in a straightforward manner; but south of Fiordland the opposite occurs, with the Pacific Plate being pushed over the Indian-Australian Plate. In between, along the great Alpine Fault of the western South Island, the plates are grinding past each other. All this shearing action has contributed to New Zealand's twisted shape.

ULTRAMAFIC AND BASALTIC VOLCANOES: Long before the New Zealand landmass was formed – as much as 300 million years ago – these forces were at work along the plate boundary in the ocean floor. A volcanic arc probably then existed on the sea floor, and some time in the Permian (280-225 million years ago) these volcanic rocks were uplifted, together with a great slice of oceanic crust and mantle, in massive earth movements that eventually led to the creation of a large landmass on the site of modern New Zealand. The rock that welled up from deep in the mantle is often called ultramafic, and it has a most unusual composition compared with our typical 'acid' rocks (such as greywacke, schist or granite). Today, the ancient remnants of this mantle and oceanic crust can be seen in two striking mountain complexes – the Dun Mountain/Red Hills belt of Nelson and the Wairau valley, and Red Mountain in the Olivine region of south Westland. The high iron content of these ultramafic rocks has 'rusted' to give the dun or red colour so characteristic of each area. In addition, the amount of magnesium (and probably other toxic elements such as nickel and chromium) in the soils derived from the rocks has meant that both areas are largely devoid of forest. However, each mountain range does carry an unusual assemblage of shrubs and herbs ('serpentine scrub'), some of them endemic to these highly mineralised regions. Both are outstanding areas of scenic and scientific importance. The reason why these two regions are today separated by 450 km lies also in 'plate tectonics'. As the two plates have slid past each other along the Alpine Fault, this zone of ultramafic rock has been gradually torn apart over the past 120-140 million years. Similarly, the granites of Fiordland and north-west

◁ RUAPEHU
This mountain dominates the volcanic landscape in the centre of the North Island. In its shadow lies the inhospitable Rangipo Desert – Te Onetapu ('the sacred sands'), in Maori lore a fearsome place for the traveller. From this volcanic centre flow the major rivers of the North Island: Wanganui and its tributaries Whakapapa and Manganui-a-te-ao, Mangawhero, the sulphurous Whangaehu, and (shown here) the stream that is the source of the mighty Waikato.

LAYERS OF ASH
Soil scientists have now gone a long way towards unravelling the remarkable chronology of tephras (airfall ash and boulders) erupted in the Taupo Volcanic Zone. Within the last 20,000 years there has been a sequence of 25 major tephra eruptions, each tephra mantling earlier eruptions like layers of a cake.

Nelson were once one contiguous formation, but have been torn apart the same distance.

As New Zealand spans a plate junction, there were probably few intervals during the last 200-300 million years when volcanoes were not erupting somewhere, either on land or under the sea. These ancient volcanoes have long since disappeared through erosion. However, the basaltic volcanoes that were erupting in Banks and Otago Peninsulas during the late Miocene (about 10 million years ago) still remain as heavily eroded craters breached by the sea. The small basalt cones of Auckland are much younger, only tens of thousands of years old. They include New Zealand's outstanding example of a basaltic volcano – Rangitoto's beautiful cone in the Hauraki Gulf. Nowhere else in New Zealand can one capture the feeling of the rough lava flows (*aa*) of the 'big island' of Hawaii. On both islands, species of *Metrosideros* (our pohutukawa and the *ohia* tree of the Hawaiians) are generally the first to colonise these inhospitable lava flows, which seem to lack both soil and water. Rangitoto, although no longer active, is probably the youngest of New Zealand's volcanoes – the primary lava eruption may only have occurred as late as 1250 AD, with a more recent, smaller eruption within the last 200 years. The amazing feature of Rangitoto is that, despite its youthfulness, it supports over 200 species of native plants, most of them on the lava flows. The reason for such botanical diversity on a very simple land form is probably the combination of a subtropical, humid climate and the inherent fertility of the Rangitoto ash (and the small amount of soil that has weathered from the lava).

AA LAVA FLOWS
The aa *lava from a volcanic eruption can soon be colonised by a variety of woody prostrate shrubs* – Dracophyllum, Gaultheria, Brachyglottis *and snow totara (*Podocarpus nivalis*).*

THE TAUPO VOLCANIC ZONE: The major centre of volcanic activity during the past 2 million years has been the Taupo Volcanic Zone. In the Hikurangi Trench, about 150 km off the east coast of the North Island, the Pacific Plate has been forced under the Indian-Australian Plate, down into the mantle where it melts to give magmas of various chemical composition. As part of this process the East Cape region has been thrust up and torn away from the rest of the North Island, leaving a massive rift valley to the west – the Taupo Volcanic Zone.

The volcanoes at the northern end (White Island, Whale Island, Mt Edgecumbe) and southern end (the Tongariro volcanic centre) of the zone are not basaltic, but andesitic. The central part of the zone (the Lake Rotorua caldera and the volcanic centres of Okataina, Maroa and Lake Taupo caldera itself) is dominated by vast amounts of rhyolitic pumice. Associated with these pumice eruptions were the great flows of hot gas and ash which welded together to form huge ignimbrite sheets on either side of the central rift – Mamaku/Pureora to the west, Kaingaroa to the east.

It has been estimated that an incredible 15,000 cubic kilometres of lava and tephra (airfall ash and pumice) have been erupted from centres in this volcanic zone during the last 2 million years. This is about 15,000 times the volume of material ejected by Mt St Helens during its calamitous eruption on 18 May 1980. It is indeed small wonder that the basement rocks of greywacke and argillite have subsided more than 3,000 m below sea level along this rift valley of the Taupo Volcanic Zone.

The Taupo eruption itself, sometime between 120 and 186 AD, is thought to be the most violent rhyolitic eruption yet documented anywhere in the world. The date of 186 AD has been suggested, on new evidence that includes reference in Chinese and Roman literature to the sun and moon rising 'red as blood' because of the volcanic dust haze which must have reached the northern hemisphere. But this eruption was only the most recent in a long series of eruptions from the volcanic zone – eruptions which have scattered ash over virtually all the North Island.

The Tarawera eruption of nearly a century ago destroyed Maori settlements such as Te Wairoa village and the world-famous Pink and White Terraces. The whole south-west face of Mt Tarawera was blasted away and a chain of craters formed for a distance of 15 km. The largest of these craters was an enlarged Lake Rotomahana; the others lie in the Waimangu valley, a dynamic hydrothermal system of outstanding recreational and scientific interest.

TONGARIRO NATIONAL PARK: At the southern end of the Rotorua – Taupo rift, high above the huge explosion crater of Lake Taupo, stand three magnificent volcanoes – Tongariro, Ngauruhoe and Ruapehu (at 2,797 m, the highest point in the North Island). The three peaks were gifted to the people of New Zealand in 1887 by the paramount chief of Ngati Tuwharetoa, Horonuku Te Heu Heu Tukino. Today, they are the focal point of Tongariro National Park, a remarkable volcanic landscape preserved from exploitation for all time: to the Tuwharetoa people a sacred land where the fire kindled by their great ancestor, Ngatori-i-rangi, still burns; to the visitor, a place to wonder at the unrestrained forces of nature, to ski or climb, or to observe the many forms of plant and animal life that have evolved here over the past 2 million years.

Volcano formation began at Mt Tongariro 2-1½ million years ago, but largely ceased when it 'blew its top' to leave a truncated mountain only 1,968 m in height. Tongariro has been scarred with as many as nine craters; some, like Red Crater (site of the striking Emerald Lakes) and Te Mari Crater, have been active within the last 100-130 years. A journey across Tongariro, with its 'moon-scape' blasted by innumerable eruptions, is an unforgettable experience. Even now, the fumaroles and boiling mud pools of Ketetahi hot springs, high above bushline on the northern slopes, remind us of the power that simmers, quietly now, beneath the ashy surface.

EROSION OF VOLCANIC LANDS
*Volcanic ash and scoria is easily eroded by wind and rain. Here, above the Rangipo Desert in the 'rain-shadow' of Mt Ruapehu, only isolated bristle tussocks (*Rytidosperma setifolia*) still cling to the surface.*

The volcanic activity gradually shifted south to Ruapehu around 750,000 years ago. The jagged peaks of the 4 km wide summit – Te Heu Heu, Paretetaitonga, Ruapehu, Girdlestone, Mitre, Pyramid, and Cathedral Rocks – attest to Ruapehu's explosive history. For its summit is really made up of a series of collapsed craters. Ruapehu is a major mountain, even by South Island standards! Montane beech and podocarp forests mantle the western and southern slopes, which were protected from the blasts of the Taupo eruption. High above, the summit still carries a number of minor glaciers as well as Crater Lake, source of the huge lahar (mud flow) of 24 December 1953 which led to the tragic deaths of 151 passengers on the Wellington–Auckland express train when the Tangiwai bridge was swept away by the swollen Whangaehu River. Ruapehu also boasts one of the longest andesitic lava flows known in the world – Rangataua lava flow covered in red beech, which has descended for 14 km from a vent below Girdlestone Peak almost to the highway near Karioi. In the rain-shadow region to the east of Ruapehu lies the inhospitable Rangipo Desert, a 'desert land' scoured by wind and thunderbursts.

The active cone of Ngauruhoe (2,291 m) is the youngest of the volcanoes, formed only within the last 2,500 years. The steep slopes are streaked with many lava flows, including those associated with the spectacular eruptions of 1954, which piled up against the old eroded vent of Pukekaikiore. A magnificent panorama of these events can be obtained from the ridge on the western side of the Mangatepopo valley. This ridge is a huge old lateral moraine from the glacier which flowed down the valley during the Pleistocene glaciations. Yet the landscape below is anything but glacial now, for the terminal faces of the flows are not bluish-white ice, but black andesitic lava.

TARANAKI VOLCANIC ZONE: Taranaki appears to have been spared the cataclysmic rhyolitic eruptions of the central part of the rift system. Instead, andesitic tephra has accumulated gradually, up to 30 m in the last 100,000 years. The zone is dominated by the beautiful symmetrical cone of Mt Egmont (2,828 m) – Taranaki to the Maori people. In Maori tradition Taranaki was, along with the volcanoes Tauhara and Putauaki (now Mt Edgecumbe), one of the vanquished suitors of the beautiful Pihanga who still stands above Lake Rotoaira near her victor husband, Tongariro. In his anger, Taranaki carved out the bed of the Wanganui River and travelled up the coast to live in lonely exile.

Egmont is relatively young, only about 70,000 years old; the other two volcanoes in the area, the densely forested Kaitake and Pouakai, are older. The last significant eruption on Egmont occurred around 1755 AD and the ringplain of the mountain bears the imprint of many lahars from the steep slopes. But it is the vegetation of the Taranaki volcanoes (also preserved as a national park) that is so different from that of the other North Island volcanoes. They have a full complement of lowland plants, with the luxuriant forest on the north-west slopes of the Kaitake Range descending to within two to three kilometres of the coast. However, the lack of many subalpine and alpine plants which would normally be expected to grow there has given Mt Egmont the biological character of a 'volcanic island'. In marked contrast to the Tongariro volcanoes, beech forest is absent. The alpine flora of Egmont and Pouakai in fact contains few of the typical subalpine and alpine species of the Tongariro volcanoes; if anything, there is a closer relationship with the alpine plants of the Tararua Ranges and the Tasman Mountains of north-west Nelson.

The isolation so evident in the volcanoes of Taranaki, then, in a small way reflects the effect of isolation in the evolution of New Zealand's flora and fauna. Kaitake, Pouakai and Taranaki are truly 'an island within the ancient islands'.

RED CRATER ▷
Still erupting little more than a century ago, Red Crater is one of the younger craters on Mt Tongariro. Today it still steams, and the smell of sulphur dioxide hangs heavy in the air nearby. Plants have yet to establish themselves around the crater rim, where the ground looks dark and singed.

△
EMERALD LAKES
These mineral-rich lakes fill explosion craters near Red Crater and the rim of the Oturere valley, all within the complex summit of Mt Tongariro. It is a harsh landscape of metallic colours, devoid of the soft yellows and greens that brighten the surrounding tussock and scrub.

◁ MT EGMONT
The classical silhouette of the dormant volcano Mt Egmont signifies its violent past. It lies 150 km to the west of the Tongariro volcanic centre, beyond the dense forests and steep hills of the Wanganui River basin. Its Maori name, Taranaki, now describes the surrounding province. As a result of its long isolation, Mt Egmont can be considered biologically to be an 'alpine island'. Not only does it lack beech but also more than a hundred other subalpine plant species common to our mountain areas. Many of the mountain plants that are present show slight evolutionary differences from the same species in other mountain ranges.

△
STREAM, MT RUAPEHU
Despite the inhospitable volcanic slopes and harsh climate, alpine plants gradually establish themselves, particularly where finer material accumulates at the foot of scree slopes or in valley floors. However, the streamside vegetation is periodically obliterated through floods, avalanches or lahars (mudflows).

Pentachondra pumila
Found in the North, South, and Stewart Islands, this attractive little heath is common on the volcanic plateau. It thrives in wet places as well as the shallow, well-drained soils of the rocky mountain slopes, where its bright red fruit will catch the eye more readily than the tiny flower.
▽

Parahebe spathulata
Growing in loose stony shingle and scoria, this small prostrate plant forms little pale patches all over the alpine gravelfields of Mt Tongariro. It is confined to the volcanic plateau, the Kaimanawa Mountains, and the Kaweka and Ruahine Ranges of the North Island.
▽

WHAKAREWAREWA
Mudpools, geysers, boiling water and fumaroles (steam vents) pepper the ground at Whakarewarewa in Rotorua in the Taupo Volcanic Zone. Rain water percolates down through the soils until it reaches the underlying rock. It is then heated by the magma, and forced up, boiling hot, through cracks and fissures, to create the thermal effects for which the area is renowned. A major tourist attraction over the last century, the valley has for much longer been the home and sacred ground of the Ngatiwhakaue tribe. It was formed by a hydrothermal explosion at least 42,000 years ago.
▽

△
STEAMING CLIFFS, LAKE ROTOMAHANA
New Zealand's thermal regions today mirror in miniature the vast volcanic and geothermal activity of the past. Lake Rotomahana lies in the largest of the craters left by the devastating Tarawera eruption of 1886, and is now 30 times its pre-eruption size. The steaming cliffs around the lake are a reminder of the active geyserfield and the famous Pink and White Terraces destroyed by the eruption.

△
WAIMANGU
Lying to the west of Lake Rotomahana is a dramatic valley, often draped in steam from its active geysers and pools of boiling water. It is particularly significant as our only major unmodified geyserfield. Rotomahana was destroyed in the Tarawera eruption, and the thermal activity of the others, Wairakei, Spa, and Orakei Korako, has diminished through exploitation of the energy in the steam or by inundation through the damming of the Waikato River for the generation of hydroelectricity. An exploration of Waimangu reveals several tropical ferns and fern allies which grow in the surrounding shrubland because of the warmth of the thermal activity.

△
SILICA SPRINGS, MT RUAPEHU
A cold water spring at the source of the Waikare Stream issues from the foot of an andesitic lava flow at an altitude of 1,300 m on the north-western slopes of Mt Ruapehu. This water is super-saturated with dissolved carbon dioxide and minerals. About 100 m downstream from the spring, enough of the carbon dioxide has been lost to lower the acidity of the water and a creamy-white deposit begins to coat the bed of the stream. The term Silica Rapids has been used to describe the most spectacular part of the 250 m long deposit. Although the spring has been called Silica Springs, this is a misnomer since the whitish mineral is a very pure alumino-silicate related to the soil clay, allophane.

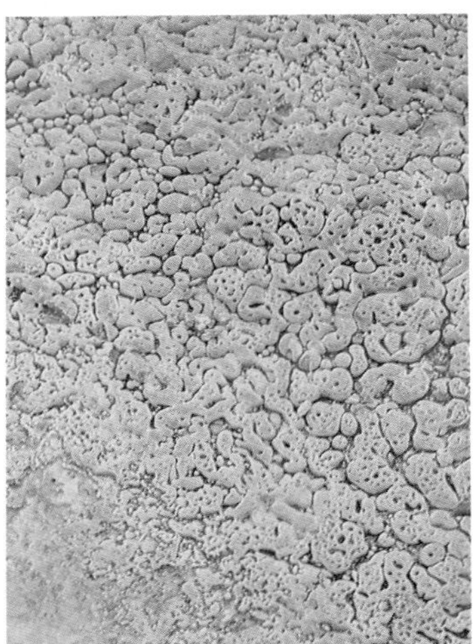

PAPAKURA GEYSER ▷
Lying almost astride the Puarenga fault in Whakarewarewa, the Papakura geyser is the most active in its series. Mineral-rich boiling water continuously sprays the surrounding ground and has created this fascinating sinter formation consisting of almost pure silica.

DETAILS OF SINTER PATTERN

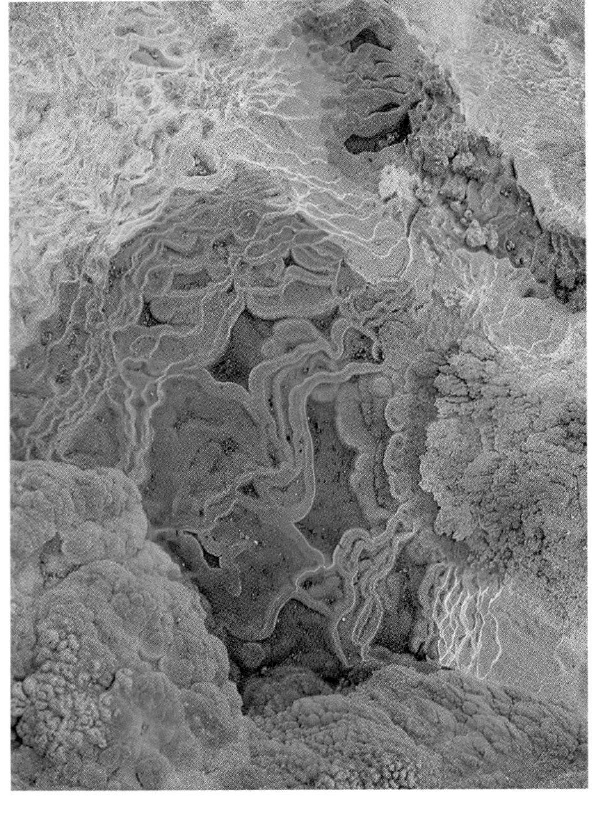

◁ BOILING MUD POOLS, WHAKAREWAREWA
The appearance and patterns of the mud pools change with the seasons. During the winter, as a result of rain, the mud is thinner and concentric patterns like those shown here form on the pools. A black oily substance (fine graphite) is also seen in some pools. In summer when the mud is thicker, small mud craters form around the openings.

Ranunculus insignis ▷
Beautiful drifts of the large yellow buttercup, *Ranunculus insignis*, can be found on the slopes of the mountains of Tongariro National Park where conditions are favourably moist (see p.118).

△
MOUNTAIN STREAM
The hard rock that forms the bed of many a small stream in the volcanic lands offers little scope for plant life. Here moss and a few lichens struggle on the rocky banks. But on the far side of the stream, wet and infertile soil characteristically supports stunted tussocks and tiny sundews.

ERODED LANDSCAPE ▷
The western slopes of Mt Ruapehu illustrate the highly erodible nature of the volcanic lands. These loosely consolidated soils have developed from numerous deposits of ejected boulders, ash and mudflows. Yet where the soils remain intact, they support a herbfield, some tussock and subalpine shrubs, and thin fingers of mountain beech reaching up into the valleys.

◁ EVERLASTING DAISY,
Helichrysum (unnamed species)
One plant that flourishes in the inhospitable environment of the alpine gravelfields is the everlasting daisy. Found throughout the mountains of the North Island, it is one of the few plants that can survive above 2,000 m on the volcanic plateau. It is also common at lower altitudes where its flowers, each on a long woolly stalk, appear in their thousands each spring and summer.

◁ BUSHLINE
A thin belt of scrub will often divide bush from tussock in New Zealand's mountains, but here, on Mt Ruapehu, the mountain beech stops abruptly where it meets the red tussock. In a volcanic landscape the bushline sometimes reflects the impact of past eruptions on the forest; in this case, however, the sharp transition probably owes more to the fires of European settlers last century when they were attempting to establish pasture on the lower slopes of these mountains.

ALGAE, SILICA SPRINGS
For the first 100m below the spring, the bed of Waikare Stream contains many colourful yellow and green algae. These cease abruptly as the alumino-silicate minerals then begin to come out of solution (see p.137).

SUBALPINE GARDEN
Huge blocks of andesitic lava shelter a garden of subalpine shrubs – *Dracophyllum recurvum*, *Brachyglottis bidwillii*, *Celmisia spectabilis* and mats of the moss *Rhacomitrium lanuginosum*.

WATERFALL, MT RUAPEHU ▷
A waterfall plunges over the edge of an old lava flow on the slopes of Mt Ruapehu. This is just one of hundreds of streams that cascade down the volcano's slopes in a series of rapids and waterfalls.

MOUNTAIN CEDAR,
Libocedrus bidwillii
The mountain cedar, or kaikawaka, is one of the most striking forest trees on the wetter western slopes of Mt Ruapehu but it does not grow on the eastern side of the volcanoes. With its deep green conical crown and tapering trunk with loose strips of reddish brown bark, the mountain cedar is a very attractive tree. It stands above a canopy of Hall's totara around 800 m on the slopes of Hauhangatahi and at higher altitudes (1,000-1,100 m) it is associated with mountain toatoa (*Phyllocladus aspleniifolius* variety *alpinus*). However, it is most widely distributed as a minor component of the extensive mountain beech (*Nothofagus solandri* variety *cliffortioides*) forest on the poorly drained ringplain of western Mt Ruapehu between 800 and 1,100 m.

Pimelea microphylla ▷
Small, sweet-scented and ground-hugging, this tiny pimelea forms mats and mounds all over the desert surface. Although the foliage is rarely more than 5 cm high, the plant has a long and thick tap root, that not only anchors the plant securely but also obtains water from the deep sand and shingle.

◁ BIDIBIDI, *Acaena novae-zealandiae*
The common bidibidi thrives on the porous volcanic soils, and is easily spread by its spherical seed heads hooking on to clothing or sheep fleeces.

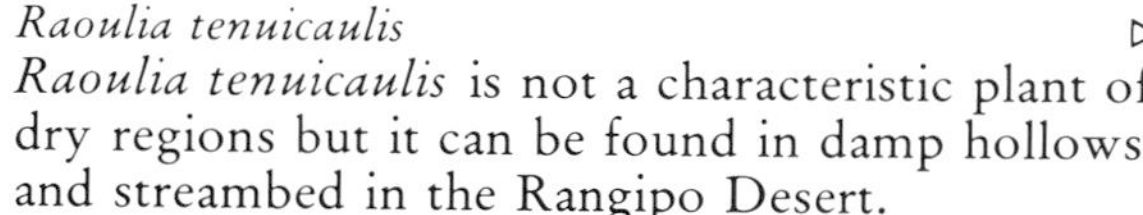

Raoulia tenuicaulis ▷
Raoulia tenuicaulis is not a characteristic plant of dry regions but it can be found in damp hollows and streambed in the Rangipo Desert.

AUSTRALASIAN HARRIER, *Circus approximans gouldi*
The harrier hawk is regularly seen soaring high above open country, where it feeds on any available animal food, dead or alive. This bird of prey is common in New Zealand, Australia and New Guinea, and even occasionally appears in the subantarctic islands.
▽

RANGIPO DESERT
The gravelfields to the east of Mt Ruapehu are a 'rain-shadow' region often called the Rangipo Desert. Yet the annual precipitation (rain plus snow) here is still quite high, around 1,200 mm, although only half the level at the same altitude on the western side of the volcano. In winter the entire landscape can be blanketed in snow or drenched with heavy rain. Strong winds rake the area in summer, continually moving sand and gravel and stirring up small 'dust devils'. Yet, even here, hardy low-growing plants such as *Pimelea microphylla*, *Carmichaelia enysii* variety *orbiculata*, *Gentiana bellidifolia* and *Raoulia albo-sericea* manage to establish themselves in the extremes of summer heat and winter cold.

BANDED DOTTEREL,
Charadrius bicinctus
Standing on top of a raoulia hump, this banded dotterel calls to its chick. The adults feign injury to try and lure the intruder away, but once the chick is safe, the adult birds retire. The dotterels breed in the Rangipo Desert during the warmer months, then migrate to the coast with the onset of winter. Their colours camouflage them superbly in this environment and only their strident call or sharp movement gives them away.

DESERTSCAPES
The effect of wind and water upon the volcanic ash and gravel is shown in these three sculptured desertscapes. In this extreme environment only the bristle tussock (*Rytidosperma setifolium*) and plants such as *Carmichaelia enysii* and *Gentiana bellidifolia* retain a tenuous hold on the land. On the more severe alpine gravelfields above 1,400 m small plants of *Oreostylidium subulatum* and *Parahebe spathulata* have colonised the fine, light volcanic gravels. These plants are well camouflaged, and only become apparent when they flower in summer. Here, too, a touch of colour can be provided in summer by the beautiful purple flower of the *Thelymitra* orchid.

◁ *Olearia nummularifolia*
Springy, tight-knit branches and thick leaves enable this olearia to survive its annual burial under winter snow. It is a feature of subalpine tussock and scrub in mountainous areas of the volcanic plateau but is found in many parts of New Zealand. The lichen is one of the species of 'old man's heard', *Usnea xanthophana*.

△
ROUGH (*AA*) LAVA
An andesitic lava flow from Mt Ngauruhoe has stopped at the foot of Pukekaikiore in the Mangatepopo valley. In places, the surface is a jumble of *aa* lava, often twisted into hideous shapes. Yet once again life has found a toehold. Mats of the grey *Raoulia albo-sericea* establish on the loose scoria; many attractive creeping herbs, including the white-flowered *Ourisia volcanica* and lavender *Parahebe hookeriana*, thrive along the banks of the Mangatepopo Stream, where sediments have accumulated from the weathering of the lava; and the tiny plants of the woody *Brachyglottis bidwillii* appear in crevices in the lava.

PLANTS ON LAVA DEBRIS ▷
Shrubs of *Dracophyllum recurvum* and mats of *Raoulia albo-sericea* eventually consolidate the areas where gravels or sands accumulate through the effect of wind and rain weathering the lava surface.

ROCK AND LICHEN ▷
Lichens slowly eat away at the surface of the andesitic rock.

SHRUB INVASION OF RED TUSSOCK GRASSLANDS
The red tussock grasslands shown below have now largely been invaded by spanish heath (*Calluna vulgaris*). The heath was introduced earlier this century as habitat for grouse which were liberated as game birds. The grouse soon died, but the heather flourished, so that the colour and character of this native grassland is fast disappearing.
▽

RED TUSSOCK GRASSLAND ▷
Away from Mt Ngauruhoe, ash and other airfall debris have gradually accumulated and smoothed out the land surface. Here, red tussock (*Chionochloa rubra*) dominates the landscape. The occasional fire caused by volcanic eruption probably maintained this type of tussock grassland, which is typical of the high, central part of the North Island. If burning had not occurred these grasslands would have gradually developed into forests of mountain toatoa and, ultimately, mountain beech.

KAKA, *Nestor meridionalis septentrionalis*
This large forest parrot is a colourful occupant of the podocarp/hardwood and beech forests on the western slopes of Mt Ruapehu. It also plays a very useful part in the life cycle of the bush, destroying insects and cross-pollinating flowers in its search for food, and dispersing seeds from the fruit it eats.

◁◁ BRUSHTAIL POSSUM, *Trichosurus vulpecula*
The Australian marsupial was first introduced to New Zealand in 1837. Today it inhabits many bush areas as well as farmland and suburban gardens. The forests of the volcanic lands, especially the podocarp/hardwood forests and any that have been cut over, are a favourite environment. Here its habit of selective browsing has caused serious damage, particularly amongst the stands of northern rata growing above Ohakune and the mistletoes of the beech forest.

◁ MOUNTAIN CABBAGE TREE, *Cordyline indivisa*
This cabbage tree, with its broad leaves and shaggy head, is characteristic of the higher forest on the volcanic plateau. It thrives in gaps in the forest canopy and its striking shape, in some ways resembling the nikau palm of warmer coastal forests, brings a hint of the subtropical into these cool mountain regions.

WATERFALL ▷
The Mangawhero River plunges over a ledge formed by an old andesitic lava flow on the western slopes of Mt Ruapehu. The scene typifies the subalpine zone on this side of the mountain – open stream beds, frequent mist and rain, and mountain beech forest with the occasional kaikawaka tree standing out.

FIGURE 3: Vegetation zones at different latitudes

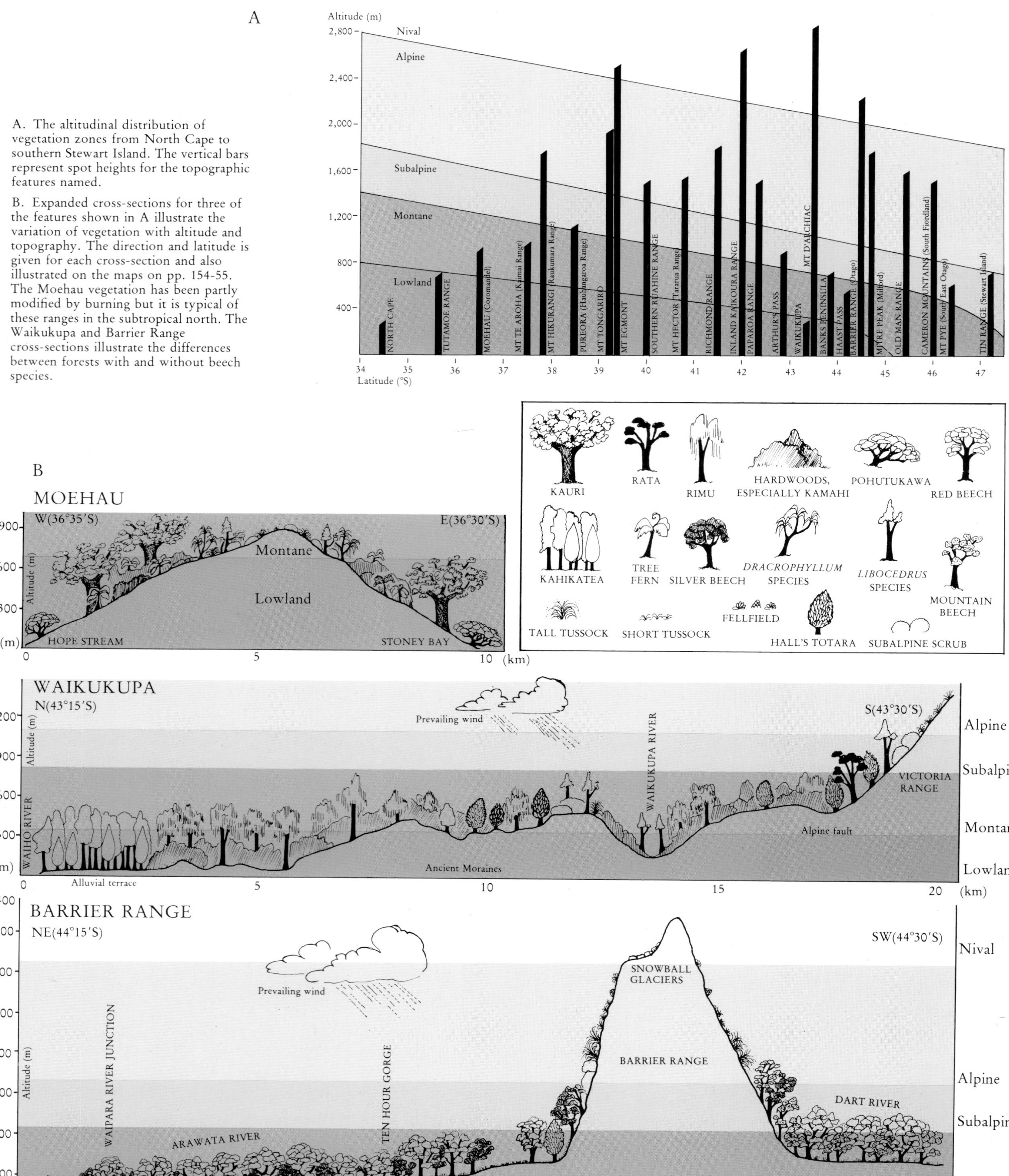

A. The altitudinal distribution of vegetation zones from North Cape to southern Stewart Island. The vertical bars represent spot heights for the topographic features named.

B. Expanded cross-sections for three of the features shown in A illustrate the variation of vegetation with altitude and topography. The direction and latitude is given for each cross-section and also illustrated on the maps on pp. 154-55. The Moehau vegetation has been partly modified by burning but it is typical of these ranges in the subtropical north. The Waikukupa and Barrier Range cross-sections illustrate the differences between forests with and without beech species.

SELECT BIBLIOGRAPHY

The following is a chapter-by-chapter list of books which deal with subjects and regions in greater detail.

1. ANCIENT NEW ZEALAND

Many scholarly essays on different aspects of New Zealand's natural history can be found in:

Kuschel, G. (ed.), 1975: *Biogeography and Ecology in New Zealand*, Junk, The Hague, 689 pp.

Williams, G. R. (ed.), 1973: *The Natural History of New Zealand: An Ecological Survey*, Reed, Wellington, 434 pp.

Some more general articles on geology, soil, climate, forestry, flora and fauna are in:

Wards, I. McL. (ed.), 1976: *New Zealand Atlas*, Government Printer, Wellington, 292 pp.

A wide range of articles on aspects of New Zealand's landforms, flora and fauna can also be found in different volumes of *New Zealand's Heritage* (Paul Hamlyn, Wellington).

GEOLOGICAL HISTORY

Fleming, C. A., 1971: 'Continents in Dispersion', pp. 12–21 in R. Knox (ed.), *New Zealand's Heritage*, Vol. 1, Pt.1, Paul Hamlyn, Wellington.

Fleming, C. A., 1979: *The Geological History of New Zealand and its Life*, Auckland University Press/Oxford University Press, 141 pp.

Stevens, G. R., 1980: *New Zealand Adrift*, Reed, Wellington, 442 pp.

A comprehensive exposition of New Zealand's geology is given in:

Suggate, R. P. (ed.), 1978: *The Geology of New Zealand*, Government Printer, Wellington, 2 vols.

and of soils in:

N.Z. Soil Bureau, 1968: *Soils of New Zealand*, N.Z. Soil Bureau Bulletin 26, Government Printer, Wellington, 3 vols.

CONSERVATION

Anon., 1979: *A Vanishing Heritage: The Problem of Endangered Species and their Habitat. Proceedings of symposium, 49th Congress Australian and New Zealand Association for the Advancement of Science (ANZAAS)*, Nature Conservation Council, Wellington, 273 pp.

G. C. Kelly, 1980: 'Landscape and Nature Conservation' in L. F. Molloy *et al* (eds.), *Land Alone Endures: Land Use and the Role of Research*, DSIR discussion paper No. 3, Wellington, pp. 63–87, presents a powerful argument for nature conservation, particularly the endemic elements in our landscape.

Given, D. R., 1981: *Rare and Endangered Plants of New Zealand*, Reed, Wellington, 154 pp.

Williams, G. R., Given, D. R. (*comp.*), 1981: *Red Data Book of New Zealand (Rare and Endangered Species of Endemic Terrestrial Vertebrates and Vascular Plants)*, Nature Conservation Council, Wellington, 175 pp.

Many other detailed treatments of aspects of New Zealand's natural history touch upon the biogeographical origins of the flora and fauna, the relationship between an organism and its environment, or habitat, and the importance of conservation measures. The following books and essays contain much useful information of this type:

FRESHWATER FISHES

McDowall, R. M., 1978: *New Zealand Freshwater Fishes: a Guide and Natural History*, Heinemann, Auckland, 230 pp.

BIRDS

Falla, R. A., Sibson, R. B., Turbott, E. G., 1979: *The New Guide to the Birds of New Zealand and Outlying Islands*, Collins, Auckland, 247pp.

Moon, G. J. H., 1979: *The Birds Around Us: New Zealand Birds, their Habits and Habitats*, Heinemann, Auckland, 207 pp.

REPTILES AND OTHER WILDLIFE

Bull, P. C., Whittaker, A. H., 1975: 'The Amphibians, Reptiles, Birds and other Mammals' in G. Kuschel (ed.), *Biogeography and Ecology in New Zealand*, pp. 231–76.

Hardy, G. S., Whittaker, A. H., 1979: 'The Status of New Zealand's Endemic Reptiles and their Conservation', *Forest and Bird*, 13 (4), No. 214, pp. 34–39.

Crook, I. G., 1975: 'The Tuatara' in G. Kuschel (ed.), *Biogeography and Ecology in New Zealand*, pp. 331–52.

O'Brien, C., 1981: *AA Book of New Zealand Wildlife: a Guide to the Native and Introduced Animals of New Zealand*, Lansdowne, Auckland, 161 pp.

PLANTS

Cockayne, L., 1967: *New Zealand Plants and their Story* (4th edn., ed. E. J. Godley), Government Printer, Wellington, 269 pp.

2. ISLAND SANCTUARIES

Atkinson, J. A. E., Bell, B. D., 1973: 'Off-shore and Out-lying Islands' in G. R. Williams (ed.), *The Natural History of New Zealand*, pp. 372–92.

3. COASTAL MARGINS

Morton, J. E., Miller, M. C., 1968: *The New Zealand Sea-shore*, Collins, London, 638 pp.

Brodie, J. W., 1973: 'The Ocean Environment' in G. R. Williams (ed.), *The Natural History of New Zealand*, pp. 61–92.

Morton, J. E., 1973: 'The Sea-shore' in G. R. Williams (ed.), *The Natural History of New Zealand*, pp. 93–130.

Morton, J., Thom, D., Locker, R., 1973: *Seacoast in the Seventies: The Future of the New Zealand Shoreline*, Hodder and Stoughton, Auckland, 118 pp.

Tortell, P. (ed.), 1981: *New Zealand Atlas of Coastal Resources*, Government Printer, Wellington.

4 & 7. THE LIVING FOREST/TOWARDS THE BUSHLINE

Wardle, P., 1964: 'Facets of the Distribution of Forest Vegetation in New Zealand', *N.Z. Journal of Botany*, 2 (4), pp. 352–66.

Godley, E. J., 1975: 'Flora and Vegetation' in G. Kuschel (ed.), *Biogeography and Ecology in New Zealand*, pp. 177–229.

Fleming, C. A., 1977: 'The History of Life in the New Zealand Forests', *N.Z. Journal of Forestry*, 22 (2), pp. 249–62. (Reprinted in *Forest and Bird*, No. 210, November 1978, pp. 2–10.)

Mark, A. F., 1977: *Vegetation of Mount Aspiring National Park, New Zealand*, National Parks Authority, Wellington, 79 pp.

Moore, L. B., Irwin, J. B., 1978: *The Oxford Book of New Zealand Plants*, Oxford University Press, Wellington, 256 pp.

Wardle, P., 1979: *Plants and Landscape in Westland National Park*, National Parks Authority, Wellington, 168 pp.

Salmon, J. T., 1980: *The Native Trees of New Zealand*, Reed, Wellington, 384 pp.

5. DIMINISHING WETLANDS

Hamilton, L. S., Hodder, A. P. W. (eds.), 1979: *Symposium on New Zealand Peatlands*, Centre for Continuing Education/Environmental Studies Unit, University of Waikato, Hamilton.

McCraw, J. D., Cheyne, J., Thompson, K., 1979: 'Peatlands in New Zealand', *Soil and Water*, 15 (4), pp. 13–21.

Thompson, K., 1979: 'The Status of New Zealand's Wetlands and Peatlands', pp. 65–89 in *A Vanishing Heritage: The Problem of Endangered Species and their Habitat*, Nature Conservation Council, Wellington.

6. TUSSOCK COUNTRY

Connor, H. E., MacRae, A. H., 1969: 'Montane and Subalpine Tussock Grasslands in Canterbury' in G. A. Knox (ed.), *The Natural History of Canterbury*, Reed, Wellington, pp. 169–204.

McCraw, J. D., 1965: 'Landscapes of Central Otago' in R. G. Lister and R. P. Hargreaves (eds.), *Central Otago*, N.Z. Geographical Society, Misc. Series No. 5, pp. 30–45.

Mark, A. F., 1965: 'Vegetation and Mountain Climate' in R. G. Lister and R. P. Hargreaves (eds.), *Central Otago*, pp. 69–91.

Mark, A. F., 1980: 'A Disappearing Heritage – Tussock Grasslands of the South Island Rain-shadow Region', *Forest and Bird*, 13 (8), No. 218, pp. 18–24.

8. ALPINE GARDENS

Wardle, P., 1968: 'Evidence for an Indigenous Pre-quaternary Element in the Mountain Flora of New Zealand, *N.Z. Journal of Botany*, 6 (1) pp. 120–25.

Mark, A. F., Adams, N. M., 1973: *New Zealand Alpine Plants*, Reed, Wellington, 262 pp.

Raven, P. H., 1973: 'Evolution of Subalpine and Alpine Plant Groups in New Zealand', *N.Z. Journal of Botany*, 11 (2), pp. 177–200.

Wardle, P., 1978: 'Origin of the New Zealand Mountain Flora, with Special Reference to Trans-Tasman Relationships', *N.Z. Journal of Botany*, 16 (4), pp. 535–50.

9. THE VOLCANIC LANDS

N.Z. Geological Survey, 1960: *Volcanoes of Tongariro National Park*, N.Z. DSIR Information Series No. 28, 82 pp.

Neall, V. E., 1976: 'Vulcanology of Egmont National Park', pp. 56–62 in J. H. Fullarton (ed.), *Egmont National Park Handbook*, 3rd edn., Egmont National Park Board, New Plymouth, 85 pp.

Delveceny, P. (ed.), 1981: *The Restless Land: The Story of Tongariro National Park*, Tongariro National Park Board, 112 pp.

NEW ZEALAND
Norfolk I (Australia)
KERMADEC IS
Raoul I
Macauley I
Curtis I
L'Esperance Rock
Three Kings Is
NORTH ISLAND
SOUTH ISLAND
Chatham Is
Stewart I
Snares Is
Bounty Is
Antipodes Is
Auckland Is
Campbell I
Kilometres 100 0 200 400
Miles 100 0 200
TASMAN SEA
Farewell Spit
Golden Bay
Stephens I
D'Urville I
TASMAN BAY
MARLBOROUGH SOUNDS
COOK STRAIT
TASMAN MTS
Heaphy Bluff
Karamea
NELSON
Dun Mtn
RICHMOND RA
BLENHEIM
Wairau R
WESTPORT
Buller R
MATIRI RA
L Rotoroa
L Rotoiti
MARLBOROUGH
PAPAROA RA
VICTORIA RA
Maruia R
SPENSER MTS
Molesworth
INLAND KAIKOURA RA
SEAWARD KAIKOURA RA
Clarence R
Kaikoura
Grey R
Lewis Pass
GREYMOUTH
L Brunner
Hokitika
Hokitika R
Taramakau R
WESTLAND
Arthur's Pass
Waitaha R
Wanganui R
Whataroa R
L Ianthe
Harihari
Okarito Lag
Waiho R
Franz Josef Gl
Mapourika
Whitcombe Pass
CRAIGIEBURN RA
Waipara R
Waikukupa Forest
Fox Gl
SOUTHERN ALPS
Mt d'Archiac
CANTERBURY
Waimakariri R
CHRISTCHURCH
Mt Cook
L Paringa
CANTERBURY PLAINS
BANKS PENINSULA
Haast
Jackson Bay
L Tekapo
Rakaia R
L Pukaki
Haast Pass
L Ohau
MACKENZIE COUNTRY
Rangitata R
Red Mtn
Arawata R
Martins Bay
L McKerrow
Mt Aspiring
TIMARU
BARRIER RA
L Wanaka
L Hawea
Ahuriri R
Milford Sd
DARRAN MTS
HUMBOLDT MTS
Hollyford R
Dart R
Mt Earnslaw
Lindis Pass
Mitre Peak
OTAGO
HAWKDUN RA
PISA RA
L Wakatipu
DUNSTAN MTS
Manuherikia R
IDA RA
Dansey Pass
Waitaki R
Queenstown
KAKANUI MTS
OAMARU
MURCHISON MTS
Alexandra
ROUGH RIDGE
Maniototo Basin
Secretary I
Doubtful Sd
L Te Anau
EYRE MTS
GARVIE MTS
OLD MAN RA
L Roxburgh
ROCK & PILLAR RA
SOUTH ISLAND
FIORDLAND
Te Anau
Wilmot Pass
L Manapouri
SOUTHLAND
Great Moss Swamp
Resolution I
TAKITIMU MTS
UMBRELLA RA
LAMMERLAW RA
Mossburn
Otago Pen
CAMERON MTS
DUNEDIN
Taieri R
Gore
Tuatapere
Clutha R
INVERCARGILL
Mt Pye
Waituna Lag
FOVEAUX STRAIT
Solander I
Catlins Coast
Codfish I
Mt Anglem
STEWART ISLAND
TIN RA
Big South Cape I
SCALE 1 : 3 200 000
Kilometres 20 0 20 40 60 80 100
Miles 20 0 20 40 60 80
168°
170°
172°
174°
40°
42°
44°
46°

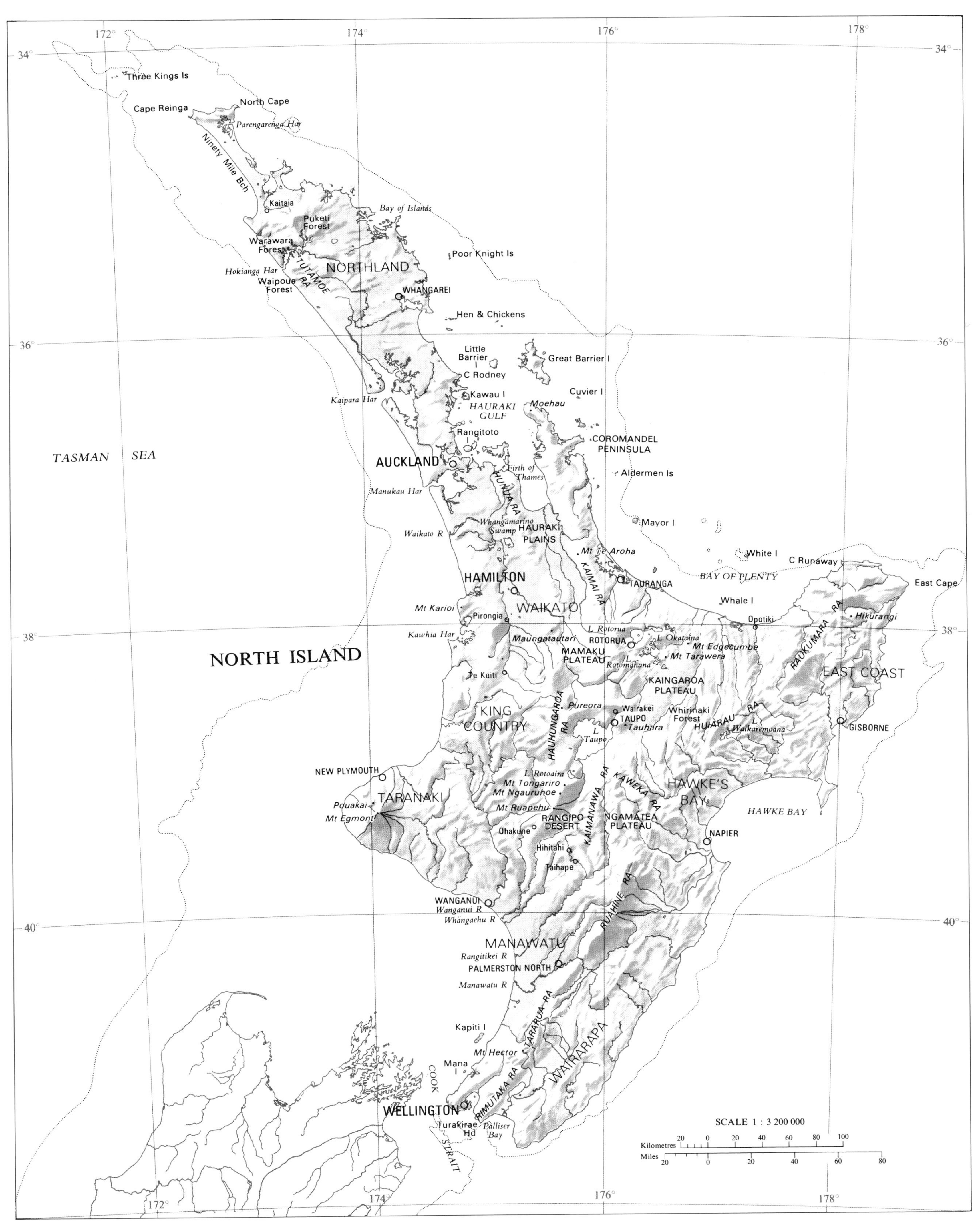

NORTH ISLAND
TASMAN SEA
Three Kings Is
North Cape
Cape Reinga
Parengarenga Har
Ninety Mile Bch
Kaitaia
Bay of Islands
Puketi Forest
Warawara Forest
Poor Knight Is
Hokianga Har
TUTAMOE RA
NORTHLAND
Waipoua Forest
WHANGAREI
Hen & Chickens
Little Barrier I
Great Barrier I
C Rodney
Cuvier I
Kawau I
Kaipara Har
HAURAKI GULF
Moehau
Rangitoto I
COROMANDEL PENINSULA
AUCKLAND
Firth of Thames
Aldermen Is
Manukau Har
HUNUA RA
Whangamarino Swamp
HAURAKI PLAINS
Mayor I
Waikato R
Mt Te Aroha
White I
C Runaway
KAIMAI RA
HAMILTON
TAURANGA
BAY OF PLENTY
East Cape
Whale I
Mt Karioi
Pirongia
WAIKATO
Opotiki
Hikurangi
RAUKUMARA RA
Kawhia Har
L Rotorua
ROTORUA
L Okataina
Maungatautari
Mt Edgecumbe
MAMAKU PLATEAU
L Rotomahana
Mt Tarawera
EAST COAST
Te Kuiti
KAINGAROA PLATEAU
HAUHUNGAROA RA
Pureora
Wairakei
Whirinaki Forest
KING COUNTRY
TAUPO
Tauhara
HUIARAU RA
L Waikaremoana
GISBORNE
L Taupo
NEW PLYMOUTH
L Rotoaira
KAWEKA RA
Mt Tongariro
HAWKE'S BAY
TARANAKI
Mt Ngauruhoe
Pouakai
Mt Ruapehu
KAIMANAWA RA
HAWKE BAY
Mt Egmont
RANGIPO DESERT
NGAMATEA PLATEAU
Ohakune
NAPIER
Hihitahi
Taihape
RUAHINE RA
WANGANUI
Wanganui R
Whangaehu R
MANAWATU
Rangitikei R
PALMERSTON NORTH
Manawatu R
TARARUA RA
Kapiti I
Mt Hector
WAIRARAPA
Mana I
COOK STRAIT
RIMUTAKA RA
WELLINGTON
Turakirae Hd
Palliser Bay
SCALE 1 : 3 200 000
Kilometres 20 0 20 40 60 80 100
Miles 20 0 20 40 60 80
172°
174°
176°
178°
34°
36°
38°
40°

GLOSSARY

ALGAE: photosynthetic plants, including seaweeds and their freshwater allies; almost all aquatic
ALLUVIAL: deposited by rivers
AMPHIBIANS: animals (such as frogs) which are adapted for life either on land or in water
ANDESITIC: volcanic rock of intermediate (between 'basic' and 'acidic') chemical composition
ARAUCARIAN: conifers of the Araucariaceae family, including kauri (*Agathis*), monkey-puzzle and Norfolk pine trees
ARGILLITE: a dark, compact rock hardened (under pressure) from mudstone sediments; often found in bands with greywacke
BASALT: volcanic flow rock of 'basic' (i.e. high in content of iron, manganese and magnesium) composition, lacking quartz
BIOGEOGRAPHY: study of the distribution of plants and animals, now and in the past
BIOTA: the plants and animals of a given region
BIVALVES: animals (usually aquatic), such as clams, oysters, scallops and mussels, which have a shell composed of two distinct, moveable parts
CANOPY: topmost continuous layer of foliage in a forest
CHLOROPHYLL: a green pigment in the leaves of green plants which is capable of absorbing the energy from sunlight to enable the plant to build up sugars (see PHOTOSYNTHESIS)
CIRQUE: amphitheatre-shaped head of a glaciated valley
CONIFERS: a group of cone-bearing trees, including kauri, podocarps, *Phyllocladus* and *Libocedrus* (mountain cedar)
CONTINENTAL SHELF: relatively shallow belt of sea-bottom bordering a continental mass, usually to a water depth of 200 m
ECOLOGICAL NICHE: a space for an organism to occupy when colonising a community
ECOLOGY: the study of the relationship of plants and animals to their environment
ECOSYSTEM: a natural system formed by the interaction of organisms with their environment; the system can be of any size
EMBRYO: a young organism in the very early stage of development
ENDEMIC: restricted to a certain region, or part of a region
EPIPHYTE: a plant which lives upon the surface of other plants
EVOLUTION: the gradual development of organisms from pre-existing organisms since the dawn of life; sometimes also used to describe the development of landforms
FAN: the fan-shaped alluvial deposit of a stream where it issues from a gorge onto a larger valley or plain
FAUNA: animal population of a given area
FELLFIELD: upper part of the alpine zone generally consisting of scattered small herbs and tussocks
FLOOD-PLAIN: an alluvial plain bordering a river, the surface of which is formed (and destroyed) by the accumulation (and removal) of deposits during floods
FOOD-CHAIN: chain of organisms through which energy is transferred; each organism obtains its energy by consuming an organism lower on the chain, the beginning of the chain being green plants
FROST-HEAVE: the raising of the soil surface through the expansion of ice in the underlying soil
GLACIAL TERRACE: a terrace of glacial origin
GLACIER: river of ice descending from a snowfield or mountain
GENUS (pl. GENERA): a subdivision of a family of organisms that contains a number of closely related species
GNEISS: a coarsely crystalline rock with layers containing mica alternating with granite-like layers; formed through metamorphism of either igneous or sedimentary rocks
GONDWANALAND: ancient supercontinent that existed in the southern hemisphere up to Triassic–Jurassic times; contained precursors of modern South America, Africa, Madagascar, India, Australia, Antarctica and New Zealand
GRANITE: a granular, crystalline rock of igneous origin, consisting essentially of quartz, feldspar and mica; of 'acidic' composition (i.e. high in silica content)
GREYWACKE: the characteristic sediments deposited in ancient ocean basins; sand-sized grains subsequently hardened into a greyish rock; contains quartz and feldspars as well as minerals of volcanic origin
HABITAT: the environment in which a particular plant or animal usually lives
HANGING VALLEY: a higher side branch of a mountainous river system now usually connected by a waterfall or series of rapids; origin of the valley is generally glacial (a smaller, feeder glacier)
HERBFIELD: lower parts of the alpine zone; a dense community of alpine herbs, usually with the addition of shrubs and tussock grasses
HERBIVORE: an animal that eats only plants
HUMUS: decaying organic material in soil
IGNEOUS: rocks (usually crystalline) formed by the cooling of magma on, or beneath, the earth's surface
IGNIMBRITE: sheets of a glassy volcanic rock formed by the welding together of extremely hot particles of rhyolitic ash during volcanic eruptions; the name means 'fire-rock'
INDIGENOUS: native to a particular region or country
INVERTEBRATES: animals without a backbone (e.g. insects, worms, snails, jellyfish)
LAHAR: a volcanic mudflow
LANDFORM: an element of the land-surface characterised by similarity in rock-type topography or state of erosion
LAVA: rock, usually basalt or andesite, that has flowed in liquid form from a volcano or a fissure in the earth's crust
LARVAE: a stage in the development of some invertebrates, after hatching but before maturity (e.g. a caterpillar is the larval form of a butterfly)
LIANE: a climbing plant with long, twining stems; typical of tropical or subtropical rainforest
LIMESTONE: a sedimentary rock, usually consisting of calcium and magnesium carbonates
LOESS: accumulated wind-blown dust
LYCOPODS: ancient fern-like plants, including the club-mosses
MAGMA: molten rock generated within the earth
MAMMALS: animals that feed their young on milk secreted by mammary glands
MANTLE: that portion of the earth lying between the crust and the core; it begins at a depth of 5 km under the ocean crust, and 20–65 km depth under the continents, and stretches to a depth of 2900 km
MARSUPIALS: a type of mammal whose young are born at a very immature stage and develop further in their mother's pouch
MELANISM: the development of more than the normal amount of dark pigment in an animal
METAMORPHIC ROCK: rocks, such as schist, where the character of the original rock is changed by the effect of heat and pressure
MICA: crystalline minerals, shiny and forming very thin flakes
MONOTREMES: a primitive type of mammal that lays eggs but also provides its young with milk (e.g. platypus)
MONTANE FOREST: forest lying within the montane zone – i.e. the middle altitude belt lying above the lowlands but below the subalpine regions
MORAINE: poorly-sorted, angular pieces of rock and debris carried by a glacier and deposited at the margins ('lateral moraine'), between tongues ('medial moraine'), or at the lower end ('terminal moraine') of the ice
MUDSTONE: a generally soft sedimentary rock consisting of clay-sized particles
NIVAL: the zone of permanent snow and ice
OROGENY: the formation of mountains by the folding and upthrusting of the landmass
PAKIHI: a particular type of wetland found on the West Coast, South Island. Natural pakihis exhibit concentric zones of indigenous vegetation but many pakihis have been reduced to rushes and umbrella fern by periodic burning
PARASITE: organism living in, or on, another organism without being of any benefit to the host
PEAT: partly decomposed mass of vegetation usually formed in a shallow wetland
PELARGIC: living in the surface waters of the ocean as opposed to living on the sea floor
PENEPLAIN: a landform of low relief formed by prolonged erosion
PHOTOSYNTHESIS: the process by which plant cells make glucose from carbon dioxide and water by using chlorophyll as a catalyst
PHYTOPLANKTON: small plants that float and drift in surface waters of the oceans
PLATE TECTONICS: the theory that the earth's crust consists of a small number of rigid plates, bounded either by mid-ocean rises where new crust is created or by subduction zones (such as ocean trenches) where the crust is subducted below the adjacent continents
PODOCARPS: the group of southern conifers including the genera *Dacrydium, Podocarpus* and *Dacrycarpus*; the name means 'fleshy fruit' in reference to the fleshy stalks of the fruits
PREDATORS: animals that prey upon other animals
QUARTZ: crystalline silica, a hard glassy-looking mineral
'RAIN-SHADOW' REGION: an area with a relatively low annual precipitation due to sheltering by a mountain range from the prevailing rain-bearing winds
RATITE BIRDS: an order of birds lacking a keel on their breastbone where flight muscles are usually attached; they are all virtually flightless and include the moa and kiwi as well as the Australian emu and ostrich
REFUGIA: an area that serves as a refuge for plants and animals, usually during a major glacial advance
RELIC: a surviving species, population or community characteristic of a time in the past
REPTILES: a class of animal that evolved to be the first vertebrates fully independent of water as a habitat; includes snakes, lizards, crocodiles and turtles
RHIZOME: an underground stem in plants, specialised from vegetative reproduction and surviving from year to year
RHYOLITIC PUMICE: a type of volcanic rock rich in silica and low in iron, manganese and magnesium; the viscous quality of rhyolitic lava leads to violent

volcanic eruptions; the lava so ejected is often full of gas bubbles and the light pale rock is termed 'pumice'

RING-PLAIN: the low-angle plain surrounding a typical basaltic or andesitic volcano, built up by successive lava flows and lahars

RODENT: mammals so called because of their habit of gnawing or nibbling (strong incisor but no canine teeth); includes rats and mice

SANDSTONE: a sedimentary rock consisting of compressed sand-sized particles, usually quartz

SCHIST: a type of metamorphic rock (a rock altered by heat and pressure); various forms of mica appear as characteristic silver flecks in the rock

SCREE: a loose sloping pile of rock fragments eroded from a cliff or mountain face and accumulated at the base of the cliff; sometimes called *talus* slopes

SEDIMENTARY ROCKS: rocks formed from layers of sediment, often including shells of marine organisms; limestone and sandstone are typical sedimentary rocks

SERPENTINE: ultrabasic rocks that have undergone metamorphosis to give greenish rocks with a greasy appearance; the vegetation of such areas is very stunted and is often termed 'serpentine scrub'

SILT: fine soil particles, between clay and sand in size (i.e. 0.002–0.05 mm in diameter)

SILTSTONE: a sedimentary rock consisting of silt-sized particles

SOIL ORGANIC MATTER: the organic fraction of the soil, consisting of plant, animal and microbial residues and the more resistant humic substances

SOLIFLUCTION: the slow downhill movement of soil and scree as a result of alternate freezing and thawing

SPECIES: a natural grouping of organisms all of which are capable of interbreeding to give similar offspring

TEPHRA: a collective term for all material, regardless of size, ejected through the air by a volcano

TOR: a mass of residual rock capping a hill after exposure by erosion

ULTRAMAFIC ROCK: an igneous rock consisting of minerals, such as olivine, with high levels of iron and magnesium and low levels of silica; serpentine and ores of nickel and chromium are often associated with occurrences of these rocks

VASCULAR PLANTS: higher plants, containing vessels which conduct fluid, e.g. xylem (water-conducting) and phloem (food-conducting) cells

WEST WIND DRIFT: wide belt of surface waters in the Southern Ocean moving east under influence of dominant westerly winds

ZOOPLANKTON: small animals that float and drift in surface waters of the oceans

PHOTOGRAPHIC NOTES

For me, the study of natural history is one long adventure that will probably span my life. It combines the thrill of learning new truths with the excitement and awe of seeing new places and species for the first time.

Natural history photography has the advantage that we can collect our 'trophies' without damaging or killing our subjects. This must appeal to anyone genuinely interested in the natural world.

It has, however, the disadvantage of requiring a lot of equipment. The methods used in taking the photographs for this book are noted below. But we should always remember that still photography records only one moment of time. The scent, sound, movement and touch of the original situation is lost when we look at the finished photograph. In order to overcome some of these inherent shortcomings, great care has been taken to photograph all subjects in their natural surroundings, or, when this was impossible, to duplicate these natural conditions as closely as possible.

My objective is not only to capture a realistic image of a subject but also to do so in a way that is aesthetically pleasing. The photographs that follow are steps towards achieving this goal. I hope that, in sharing them, readers may be brought in closer contact with nature itself and that we may all pause to consider for a moment the wonder of creation.

Brian Enting

For all these photographs, Kodak transparency film has been used:

High Speed Ektachrome	160ASA
Ektachrome X	64ASA
Ektachrome 200	200ASA
Ektachrome 64	64ASA
Kodachrome 64	64ASA
Kodachrome 25	25ASA
Tungsten 160	160ASA

At times the speed of professional film was manipulated to allow for the use of telephoto lenses at low light levels. Where light levels made photography impossible, electronic flash was used. Natural light was always preferred. In most cases film was kept refrigerated between expeditions and between exposure and processing.

Several cameras were used:

Nikonos – Underwater camera
Veriwide – 120 format
Widelux – 35 mm traversing lens
Nikon F
Nikon F2AS Photomic

Most of the photographs were taken on the Nikon F using the following lenses:

Nikkor 28 mm 3.5
Micro Nikkor 55 mm f 2.8
Nikkor 80–200 mm Zoom f 4.5
Nikkor 300 mm f 4.5
Reflex Nikkor 500 mm f 8
(Polarising, U.V. and skylight filters were used on occasion.)

A tripod or Rowi lowpod was often used to steady telephoto lenses or when shooting close ups with the Micro Nikkor.

Other equipment included:

Nikon SR–2 Ring Flash
Sunpak 3,000
Sunpak 3,400
Mecablitz 60CT–1 and Mecablitz 60–40
Mecablitz Televorsatz
Mecablitz Mecamat 60–30
Calcu-Flash digital flash meter

For aerial photographs, 5Y or 10Y gelatine filters were applied to the lenses to reduce blue casts.

On long trips into the hills, this list of equipment was usually reduced to one camera and two lenses, while for shorter trips and one day rambles, a much greater amount of gear was carried. When possible gear was carried in containers lined with sponge rubber.

Frequent lens cleaning, dusting and maintenance are routine. As some light meters malfunction in freezing conditions, a separate one (Sekonic Viewmeter L-206) was carried to check occasional exposures.

When photographing animals and plants, especially rare ones, great care was taken to preserve both the species and its habitat. On occasion, opportunities were passed up rather than risk disturbing species and subsequently jeopardising their chances of survival.

The huias and laughing owl are museum specimens, photographed in the studio because they are considered extinct.

p. 1	LICHEN AND ALGAE: Micro Nikkor lens, hand held
pp. 2-3	GIANT PETREL: 300 mm Nikkor, hand held
p. 4	DROSERA AURICULATA: Micro Nikkor, tripod, M2 ring natural light
p. 8	SILVER FERN: 80-200 mm Zoom Nikkor hand held
p. 10	PERIPATUS: Micro Nikkor
p. 11	HOCHSTETTER'S FROG: simulated conditions, Micro Nikkor, ring flash, assisted by Dr B. Bell
	NATIVE LAND SNAIL: Micro Nikkor, hand held
p. 12	BLACK STILT: 300 mm Nikkor, tripod
	TUATARA: Micro Nikkor, ring flash
p. 13	FALLOW DEER: 80-200 Zoom Nikkor, hand held
p. 14	LAUGHING OWL: Museum specimen, tungsten film, tripod, Micro Nikkor
	HUIAS: Micro Nikkor, studio, tungsten film
p. 15	REDFINNED BULLY: specially constructed tank with flowing water, Micro Nikkor, flash
	PRIMAEVAL FOREST: widelux 35 mm camera with traversing lens, tripod
p. 16	LONG ISLAND: Aerial, 80 mm Nikkor, 10Y Filter, Ultraviolet Filter L37c
p. 17	A RARE SPECIES: Micro Nikkor, tripod
p. 18	SHORE PLOVER: Controlled situation, standard lens, natural light
p.19	EUROPEAN STOAT: Nikkor, flash, hand-held
p. 20	TARANGA ISLAND: 300 mm Nikkor, tripod
	PIED SHAGS: 500 mm reflex Nikkor, tripod
p. 21	PIED SHAGS: (drying wings): 300 mm Nikkor, tripod
p. 22	LITTLE BARRIER: Veriwide, tripod
	PYRROSIA FERN: Micro Nikkor, hand-held
	SUMMIT RIDGES: standard lens
p. 23	COOK'S PETREL: standard lens, flash (Mecablitz 60CT-1)
	AWAROA STREAM: Veriwide, tripod
	BLACK PETREL: standard lens, flash (Mecablitz 60CT-1)
	BROOM: Micro Nikkor, tripod

pp. 24-25 BOULDER BEACH: Veriwide, tripod
p. 26 CHATHAM ISLAND FORGET-ME-NOT: Micro Nikkor, tripod
CHATHAM ISLAND ICE PLANT: Micro Nikkor, tripod
p. 27 HOKATAKA: Micro Nikkor, tripod
EUPHORBIA GLAUCA: Veriwide, tripod
p. 28 POHUTUKAWA FLAT: Veriwide, hand-held
CHATHAM ISLAND YELLOW-CROWNED PARAKEET: 80-200 Zoom Nikkor
STITCHBIRD: 80-200 Zoom Nikkor, flash
p. 29 HAMILTON'S FROG: Micro Nikkor, ring flash
KIORE: Micro Nikkor, flash (Mecablitz 60CT-1)
DUVAUCEL'S GECKO: Micro Nikkor, hand-held
p. 30 HAURAKI GULF: Veriwide, tripod
p. 31 ROCKY COASTLINE: Veriwide, tripod
p. 32 OYSTERCATCHER: 500mm Reflex Nikkor, tripod
p. 33 MANGROVES: Veriwide, tripod
p. 34 SOUTHERN BLACK-BACKED GULLS: 300mm Nikkor, hand-held, 1/1000sec
p. 35 FUR SEAL: 500mm Reflex Nikkor, tripod, low angle by standing in water
BLUE PENGUIN: Nikonos underwater camera, 35mm lens
p. 36 KAREKARE: Veriwide, tripod
DEAD FISH: Micro Nikkor
p. 37 BULL KELP: Veriwide, tripod
FLOTSAM: Standard lens, hand-held
p. 38 WHITE-FRONTED TERN: 500mm Reflex Nikkor, tripod
p. 39 COASTAL VEGETATION: Standard lens, hand-held
REEF HERON: 300mm Nikkor, tripod, photograph as last in series taken in tidal pools
pp. 40-41 SNAPPER SCALES; WATER, SAND, SUNSET; COCKLE BANK; COASTAL BUBBLES; PAUA SHELL; TIDAL SAND FINGERS: All photographed with Micro Nikkor lens, some hand-held, some on tripod.
p. 42 ICE PLANT: Micro Nikkor
SHINGLE BEACHES: Micro Nikkor
SAND HIBISCUS: Micro Nikkor, tripod
HARESTAIL: Micro Nikkor
p. 43 GERANIUM MOLLE: Micro Nikkor, tripod
SAND DUNES: Micro Nikkor
MARRAM GRASS: Micro Nikkor
p. 44 FIXED DUNES AND DEPRESSIONS: 80-200 Zoom Nikkor
RAOULIA: Micro Nikkor
DUNEPONDS: Micro Nikkor
p. 45 MUEHLENBECKIA AXILLARIS: Micro Nikkor, tripod
COMMON COPPER BUTTERFLY: Micro Nikkor, tripod, ring flash
COPROSMA ACEROSA: Micro Nikkor, hand-held
p. 46 CORIARIA SARMENTOSA: Micro Nikkor, tripod
POMADERRIS RUGOSA: Micro Nikkor, tripod
MATATA: Micro Nikkor, tripod
p. 47 MANGROVE: Veriwide, tripod
MANGROVE ROOTS: Micro Nikkor, tripod
GLASSWORT: Micro Nikkor
CREEPING SELLIERA: Micro Nikkor
p. 48 GOLDEN AKEAKE: Micro Nikkor, M2 ring, F32, tripod
METROSIDEROS CARMINEA: Micro Nikkor
NGAIO: Micro Nikkor, tripod
POHUTUKAWA: The 110 degree range of the Veriwide was essential owing to lack of space.
p. 49 AURICULARIA POLYTRICHA: Micro Nikkor, tripod. I managed to use a tripod up this dead tree! A long exposure was needed with the aperture of f32.
p. 50 THE FOREST CYCLE: Veriwide, tripod
p. 52 FOREST EDGE: standard lens, hand-held
p. 54 LOWLAND FOREST: 80-200 Zoom Nikkor, tripod
FOREST INTERIOR: Veriwide, tripod
p. 55 DENSE PODOCARP FOREST: Veriwide, tripod
p. 56 LIMESTONE CAVE: Veriwide, tripod
FOREST EDGE: Veriwide, tripod
p. 57 KAURI SANCTUARY: Veriwide, tripod
BLECHNUM FERNS: Veriwide, tripod
p. 58 NORTH ISLAND KOKAKO: 300mm Nikkor, flash, tripod. Owing to the darkness of the bird and foliage, the lens needed to be opened two additional stops.
TORO: Micro Nikkor, M2 ring, tripod
PITTOSPORUM CORNIFOLIUM: Micro Nikkor, tripod
p. 59 NEW ZEALAND PIGEON: 300mm Nikkor, hand-supported. When using a tripod is impracticable, any other means of support is better than none at all. Here a tree-trunk helped.
LACEBARK: Micro Nikkor, tripod
PYGMY ORCHID: Micro Nikkor, tripod, M2 ring
p. 60 COCKROACH: Micro Nikkor, ring flash
CROWN FERN: Micro Nikkor
NORTH ISLAND ROBIN: 80-200 Zoom Nikkor, flash, diffusor
MOSS: Micro Nikkor, M2 ring
p. 61 FOREST FLOOR LITTER: Micro Nikkor
FILMY FERNS: Retina Reflex III
p. 62 FAIRY LAMPSHADE FUNGI: Micro Nikkor, tripod, ring flash; horizontal version, natural light
HELM'S BUTTERFLY: Micro Nikkor tripod
p. 63 KAURI BARK: Micro Nikkor
FUNGUS: Micro Nikkor, tripod, ring flash
FUNGUS ON WOOD: Micro Nikkor, ring flash, tripod
p. 64 CAVE WETA: Micro Nikkor, ring flash, tripod
GREAT SPOTTED KIWI: 80-200 Zoom Nikkor, flash
ORBWEB SPIDER: Micro Nikkor, ring flash, tripod
MALE PURIRI MOTH: Micro Nikkor, ring flash, tripod
p. 65 PALE BROWN LONGHORN BEETLE: Micro Nikkor, ring flash, tripod
MOREPORK: 300mm Nikkor, flash plus tele extender (intensifier)
WHITE PLUME MOTH: Micro Nikkor, ring flash, tripod
p. 66 WATERCOURSE IN BEECH FOREST: Veriwide, tripod
p. 67 PITTOSPORUM ELLIPTICUM: Micro Nikkor, tripod
BELLBIRD: 80-200 Zoom Nikkor, hand-held
p. 68 KIEKIE: Micro Nikkor, tripod
'GREENHOOD' ORCHID: Micro Nikkor, tripod
LICHEN: Micro Nikkor, tripod
COPROSMA GRANDIFOLIA: Micro Nikkor
MISTLETOE: Micro Nikkor, tripod
p. 69 TREE FUCHSIA: Micro Nikkor, tripod
TOROPARA: Micro Nikkor, tripod
BLACK HUNTING WASP: Micro Nikkor, tripod, ring flash, M2 ring
p. 70 SILVEREYE: Micro Nikkor, flash
GASTRODIA CUNNINGHAMII: Micro Nikkor, flash
TURUTU: Micro Nikkor, flash
p. 71 STARRED GECKO: Micro Nikkor
KATYDID: Micro Nikkor, ring flash
NORTH ISLAND PIED FANTAIL: 80-200 Zoom Nikkor, flash
pp. 72-73 MONTANE BEECH/HARDWOOD FOREST; MONTANE BEECH FOREST; BEECH FOREST; MONTANE BEECH FOREST: all these photographs were taken with the 120 Format Veriwide, with a tripod.
pp. 74-75 BEECH FOREST; BEECH SEEDLING; BEECH SAPLINGS; MATURE BEECH FOREST: all these photographs were taken on the Veriwide, except the BEECH SEEDLING, which was photographed on 35mm with the Micro Nikkor lens.
p. 76 SWAMP: Micro Nikkor, tripod
p. 77 LAKE MAPOURIKA: 80-200 Zoom Nikkor
p. 78 MONTANE BOG: Veriwide, tripod
GREAT MOSS SWAMP: Aerial photo, 80mm Nikkor, 10Y gelatine filter
PAKIHI: Veriwide, tripod
p. 79 CUSHION BOG: Veriwide, tripod
p. 80 MIRROR LAKES: Veriwide, tripod
DRAGON-FLY: 80-200 Zoom Nikkor, M2 ring, tripod
SWAMP MUSK: Micro Nikkor
LITTLE SHAG: 500mm Reflex Nikkor, tripod
p. 81 BITTERN: 80-200 Zoom Nikkor
PUKEKO: 500mm Reflex Nikkor, tripod
p. 82 POND: 28mm Nikkor
WHANGAMARINO SWAMP: Widelux (35mm film) Traversing lens
BLACK SWAN: 300mm Nikkor, tripod
PIED STILT: 300mm Nikkor, tripod
p. 83 LITTLE BLACK SHAGS: 500mm Reflex Nikkor, tripod
p. 84 NORTH ROUGH RIDGE: Veriwide, tripod
p. 85 HIGH COUNTRY SHEEP MUSTER: 200mm Vivatar lens
p. 86 SWEET BRIAR: Micro Nikkor
pp. 88-89 THE MANIOTOTO: Veriwide, tripod. This shot was taken in a fierce wind on the slopes of Mt Buster at 8.30 p.m. The tripod was kept as low as possible, one leg being held all the time to prevent the equipment from being blown over. The low light on these long summer evenings enhances the beautiful tawny colourings of the Otago tussocks.
p. 90 IDA RANGE: 300mm Nikkor, tripod
COMMON GRASS ORCHID: Micro Nikkor, tripod
IDA RANGE FOOTHILLS: Veriwide
p. 91 SUBALPINE MIST: 28mm Nikkor
GRASSHOPPER: Micro Nikkor, M2 ring, tripod
BROOM: Micro Nikkor, tripod

p. 92 CORAL BROOM: Micro Nikkor, tripod
RAGGEDY RANGE: 80mm Nikkor
BRANCHES LICHEN: Micro Nikkor, lowpod

p. 93 COMMON BROWN SKINK: Micro Nikkor
RAOULIA HOOKERI: Micro Nikkor, M2 ring, lowpod
CLUTHA VALLEY AND KNOBBY RANGE: 300mm Nikkor, tripod
HYMENANTHERA ALPINA: Micro Nikkor, lowpod

pp. 94-95 All three photographs were aerials using an 80mm Nikkor lens. This winter atmosphere was exceptionally clear. It is essential to use a plane with a window that can be opened for photography.

p. 96 BULBINELLA: Micro Nikkor, tripod
LINDIS PASS: Micro Nikkor
KAKANUI FOOTHILLS: 300mm Nikkor, tripod

p. 97 MATAGOURI: Micro Nikkor
HEADWATERS OF THE OTEMATATA RIVER: Aerial, 80mm Nikkor, 10Y filter
SUMMITS OF HAWKDUN RANGE: Aerial, 80mm Nikkor, 10Y filter

p. 98 WINTER SNOWFALL: Micro Nikkor. On this shoot, the light meter malfunctioned owing to the cold and a lot of film was lost as a result. I now carry an additional meter which I strap under protective clothing to keep it warm.

p. 99 SUBALPINE BEECH: Micro Nikkor

p. 101 SNOW TOTARA: Micro Nikkor, tripod
BLUE LAKE: 28mm Nikkor

p. 102 TRAVERS RIVER: Micro Nikkor
BEECH SAPLINGS: 28mm Nikkor

p. 103 BLUE LAKE: Micro Nikkor
RAOULIA, ALGAE, STONES: Micro Nikkor
WEST SABINE TARN: Micro Nikkor

p. 104 MOUNTAIN LACEBARK: 80-200 Zoom Nikkor
BRACHYGLOTTIS: Micro Nikkor
SUBALPINE FOREST: Veriwide, tripod

p. 105 HOLLYFORD RIVER: Veriwide, tripod
HAKEKE: Micro Nikkor, tripod
WILMOT PASS: Veriwide, tripod

p. 106 SPANIARD: 28mm Nikkor
STREAMSIDE: Veriwide, tripod

p. 107 NATURAL SUBALPINE GARDENS: Veriwide, tripod
PYGMY PINE: Micro Nikkor, tripod
INAKA: Micro Nikkor, tripod

p. 108 BRACHYGLOTTIS BIDWILLII: Micro Nikkor
MOUNTAIN FLAX: Micro Nikkor

p. 109 TAKAHE: 300mm Nikkor, flash (Mecablitz 60CT-1)
COPROSMA CILIATA: Micro Nikkor, tripod

p. 110 BEECH, LICHEN, SNOW: 28mm Nikkor
MOUNTAIN BEECH: Veriwide, tripod
ICED TWIGS: Micro Nikkor, tripod. All three photographs were taken during a snowstorm.
FROST HEAVE: Micro Nikkor, tripod

p. 111 SUBALPINE ZONE: Veriwide, tripod

p. 112 TEMPLE BASIN: Veriwide, tripod

p. 113 OTAGO ALPS: 80-200 Zoom Nikkor

p. 114 HIMALAYAN THAR: 80-200 Zoom Nikkor

p. 115 KEA: 80-200 Zoom Nikkor, (Mecablitz 60CT-1)
AN ALPINE GARDEN: Micro Nikkor

p. 116 CRAIGIEBURN RANGE: Veriwide, tripod
SNOW TUSSOCK/SHRUBLAND: Micro Nikkor

p. 117 MOUNTAIN RIDGES: Retina Reflex III
CELMISIA SEMICORDATA: Micro Nikkor
MOUNTAIN HAREBELL: Micro Nikkor
MT EARNSLAW: Vivatar 200mm

p. 118 MOUNTAIN CASCADE: Micro Nikkor
RANUNCULUS INSIGNIS: Micro Nikkor

p. 119 ANGELUS TARN: Micro Nikkor
UPPER OTIRA RIVER: Veriwide, tripod
DROSERA ARCTURI: Micro Nikkor
BLUE DUCK: 300mm Nikkor, tripod (high speed Ektachrome pushed one stop)

pp. 120-21 WINTER SNOWS: Veriwide, tripod

p. 122 SOUTH ISLAND EDELWEISS: Micro Nikkor
VEGETABLE SHEEP: Micro Nikkor

p. 123 ROCKY BENCH: Veriwide
HEBE HAASTII: Micro Nikkor

p. 124 SCREE SLOPES: Veriwide, tripod
HANGING VALLEY: Veriwide, tripod

p. 125 ANISOTOME: Micro Nikkor, lowpod
SCREE PLANTS: Micro Nikkor, lowpod
STONEFIELD DAISY: Micro Nikkor, lowpod

p. 126 SUMMIT OF OLD MAN RANGE: Veriwide, tripod

p. 127 SOUTH ISLAND PIED OYSTERCATCHER: 80-200 Zoom Nikkor
EROSION PAVEMENT: Veriwide, tripod

p. 128 ALPINE GENTIAN: Micro Nikkor, lowpod
HEBE BUCHANANII: Micro Nikkor, lowpod

p. 129 CELMISIA SESSILIFLORA: Micro Nikkor, tripod
CUSHION/HERBFIELD: Veriwide, tripod

p. 130 RUAPEHU: Veriwide

p. 131 LAYERS OF ASH: Micro Nikkor

p. 132 *AA* LAVA FLOWS: Micro Nikkor

p. 133 EROSION OF VOLCANIC LANDS: Micro Nikkor

p. 134 RED CRATER: Veriwide, tripod
EMERALD LAKES: Veriwide, tripod

p. 135 MT EGMONT: 300mm Nikkor, tripod
PENTACHONDRA PUMILA: Micro Nikkor
PARAHEBE SPATHULATA: Micro Nikkor
STREAM: Micro Nikkor

p. 136 WHAKAREWAREWA: 80-200 Zoom Nikkor, tripod
STEAMING CLIFFS: Aerial, Micro Nikkor

p. 137 WAIMANGU: Veriwide, tripod
SILICA SPRINGS: Veriwide, tripod

p. 138 DETAILS OF SINTER PATTERN: Micro Nikkor
BOILING MUD: Micro Nikkor

p. 139 PAPAKURA GEYSER: Veriwide, tripod

p. 140 RANUNCULUS INSIGNIS: Veriwide, tripod
MOUNTAIN STREAM: Veriwide, tripod

p. 141 ERODED LANDSCAPE: Micro Nikkor
EVERLASTING DAISY: Veriwide, tripod
BUSHLINE: Veriwide, tripod

p. 142 ALGAE, SILICA SPRINGS: Veriwide, tripod
SUBALPINE GARDEN: Veriwide, tripod

p. 143 WATERFALL: Veriwide, tripod
MOUNTAIN CEDAR: Micro Nikkor

p. 144 PIMELEA MICROPHYLLA: Micro Nikkor, lowpod
BIDIBIDI: Micro Nikkor, tripod
RANGIPO DESERT: Veriwide, tripod. Strong winds continually picked up dust and sand which can penetrate camera equipment and scratch film. Several times during this shoot I had to crouch on the ground to shelter from 'dust devils'.

p. 145 RAOULIA TENUICAULIS: Micro Nikkor, lowpod
AUSTRALASIAN HARRIER: 300mm Nikkor

pp. 146-47 BANDED DOTTEREL: 300mm Nikkor, tripod
OLEARIA NUMMULARIFOLIA: Micro Nikkor, tripod
DESERTSCAPES: 28mm and Micro Nikkor lenses; largest photograph, Veriwide

p. 148 ROUGH LAVA: Micro Nikkor
PLANTS ON LAVA DEBRIS: Micro Nikkor

p. 149 RED TUSSOCK GRASSLAND: 28mm Nikkor
ROCK AND LICHEN: Micro Nikkor
SHRUB INVASION: 28mm Nikkor. All these photos were taken during appalling weather. For this reason all shots are hand-held for speed and protection against rain.

p. 150 MOUNTAIN CABBAGE TREE: Veriwide, tripod
KAKA: 80-200mm Zoom Nikkor
BRUSHTAIL POSSUM: 80-200mm Zoom Nikkor, flash

p. 151 WATERFALL: Veriwide, tripod. It is fitting that this photograph should be the last. Although it was cold and wet, the mist and rain added an almost magical quality to this montane forest. I had a very successful day's shoot and felt happy that I'd captured a little of the 'magic' in this photograph.

INDEX

Species and genera only are indexed; pages with illustrations are in **bold**.